Houghton Mifflin
English

Teacher's Resources

Level 8

Houghton Mifflin Company ▪ **Boston**
Atlanta ▪ Dallas ▪ Geneva, Illinois
Palo Alto ▪ Princeton ▪ Toronto

Houghton Mifflin
English

Teacher's Resources

Credits

Front cover photograph: © *Ken Osburn*
Back cover photograph: *Jon Chomitz*
Text design and production: *Bookwrights, Inc.*

Illustrations
Marion Eldridge: 131, 150, 166
Walter Fournier: 24, 94, 130, 147
Meg Kelleher: 111, 129, 165
Bob McKillop: 93
Cheryl Piperberg: 75, 76, 77, 112, 148

Printed in U.S.A.

ISBN: 0-395-50288-8

ABCDEFGHIJ-SM-96543210/89

Table of Contents

Table of Contents

Part I: Teacher's Instructional Resources

Mapping for Reading and Writing

This section suggests ways of using maps as an aid to teaching the literature in the Student Book and as a tool in planning the types of writing in the Writing Process assignments.

Glossary of Literary Terms

This glossary is for your use in discussing literature with your students. It broadens the definitions of the terms in boldface type in the literature questions in your Student Book and provides additional examples.

Evaluating Composition

This professional essay presents specific samples and scoring guides that help make the evaluation process simpler and more effective for you.

Mapping for Reading and Writing

The words *see* and *understand* are often used as synonyms, and with good reason. Many people, and children especially, understand ideas best when they can visualize them. In the classroom, mapping enables children to see and understand the structure or pattern of the type of writing they are studying. Used in this context, the word *map* refers to a graphic representation of the relationships among the facts, ideas, or events in a piece of writing.

Current professional literature contains a variety of seemingly interchangeable terms related to mapping. Although these terms do overlap, the following definitions might be useful.

- **story map:** a map of a narrative, showing its structure and key events

- **concept map:** a map of an expository piece of writing, showing the relationships among the important ideas

- **web:** a map formatted with a word, concept, or topic in the center and related ideas connected by spokes to the center. A cluster is an example of a web.

- **semantic map:** a map or web developed from a key concept vocabulary word

Maps can be used to represent many different types of writing, and there is no one correct way to map a given type. Below are examples of maps that can be used with different types of writing.

1. STORY MAP

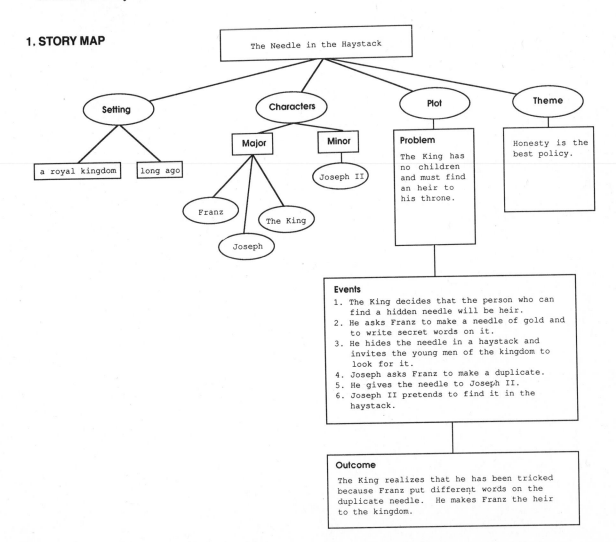

2. CONCEPT MAP:
REPORT

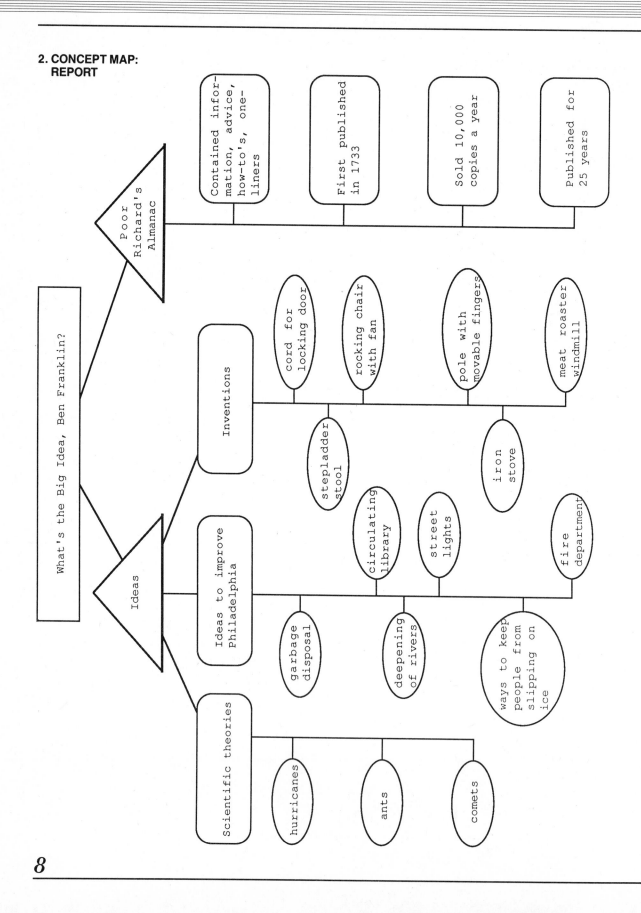

3. WEB (CLUSTER): DESCRIPTION

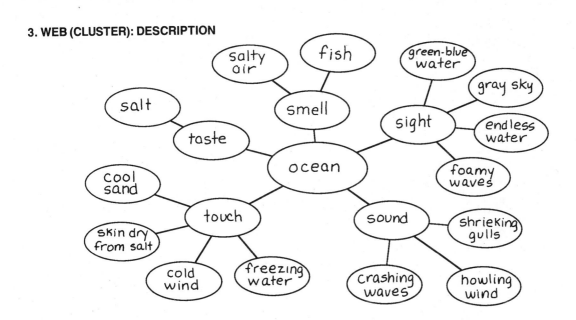

4. CONCEPT MAP: CAUSE AND EFFECT

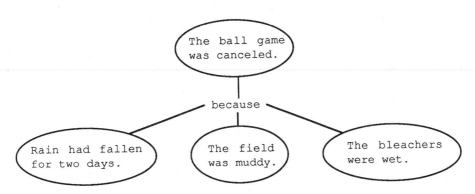

5. CONCEPT MAP: PERSUASION

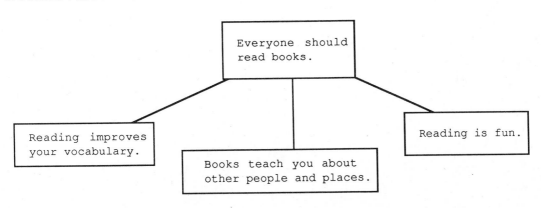

Because it has effective applications in both reading and writing, and because students seem to love it, mapping is an extremely useful technique in helping students to make the transition from reading to writing. Below are some suggestions for ways to use maps.

Before reading

As a prereading activity, mapping can be used to elicit the students' prior knowledge about the topic of a reading selection. The map gives them a framework on which to build as they read the selection.

- Introduce a selection by writing the topic on the board and drawing a box around it. Ask the class to suggest words, facts, ideas, or opinions related to the topic. Write their ideas on the board around the topic. Show the relationships among ideas by drawing a line between each idea and the topic and between any two related ideas. After the students have read the selection, have them use this map to compare their original ideas with what they have learned in their reading.

- Create a concept map or a semantic map of any vocabulary or ideas that the students should be familiar with in order to fully comprehend the selection.

After reading

A map is an excellent tool for class discussion about a reading selection. You might want to create a map to refer to when guiding discussion, or you might develop the map with the class as part of the discussion process. (See page 11 for a practice master of a blank story map.) Although mapping can also be a good individual activity, it should be assigned only after the class has used maps enough to be familiar and comfortable with them.

- When reading a narrative selection, you might create the beginning and end of a story map as a class and have the students define the key events

individually. You might also ask them to create several sets of events, each one from the viewpoint of a different character.

- Have the students create their own maps of a given selection. Then have them compare maps to see the different ways in which a selection can be interpreted. Keep in mind that since there are many ways to make maps, they should never be corrected!

- Have the students write a summary of a selection, using a completed story map or concept map as a guide.

Before writing

As a prewriting activity, mapping can be used as a way of organizing ideas within the structure of a particular type of writing. It can also be used to help students identify appropriate topics to write about.

- Have the students brainstorm or free-associate writing topics by creating clusters, or webs. Tell them to start by writing an idea in the center of a piece of paper and circling it. Then have them create branches from the center, letting one idea lead to another. Clustering is taught in your student book as part of the Writing Process.

- Have the students create concept maps before writing reports. The maps can either substitute for traditional outlines or be converted to outline form.

- Have the students make story maps before writing stories, but be sure that they use these maps as a stimulus and a guide and not as a rigid plan.

- Many of the prewriting masters included in Part III of this book are actually types of story, concept, or semantic maps. You might want to use one to map a literature selection with the class and then distribute blank copies of the same master to be used as a prewriting activity.

STORY MAP MASTER

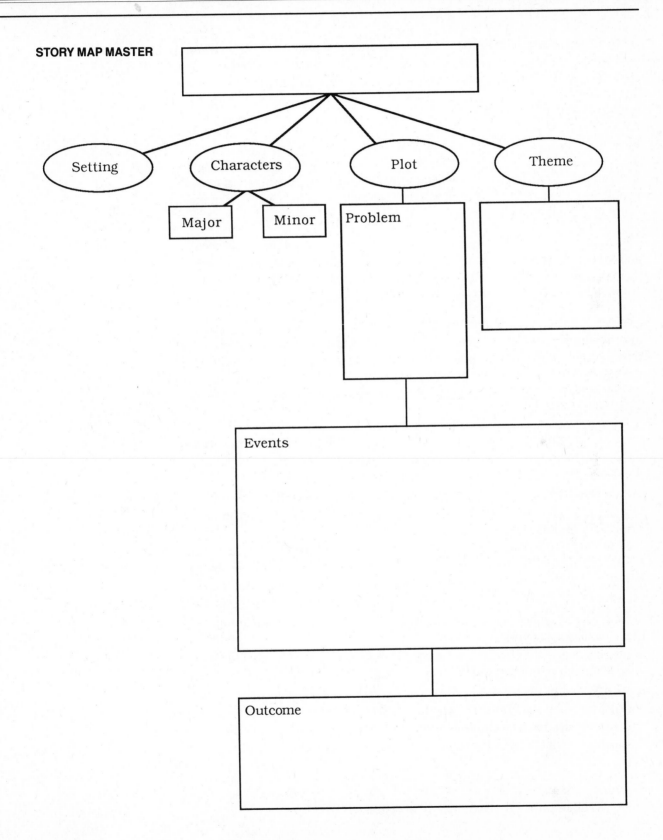

Setting

Characters

Plot

Theme

Major

Minor

Problem

Events

Outcome

Glossary of Literary Terms

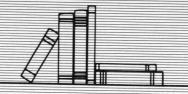

alliteration   the repetition of the same sound at the beginning of two or more words that are close together. Alliteration is a poetic device that serves to organize and unify a poem, to make it easier to memorize, and to convey the author's tone. An example of alliteration is *"Pretty Polly petted her panda / And put it in the pen."* The tone here is frivolous.

autobiography   the true story of a person's life written by the subject. An autobiography usually places emphasis on the subject's inner, private life, and in this respect is different from a *memoir,* which is usually concerned more with people and events that the author has encountered. "Growing Up" is from Russell Baker's autobiography of the same name.

characters   the people, animals, and occasionally objects or ideas that speak and act in poems, stories, novels, and plays. The main character, around whom the plot revolves, is usually the one who faces the conflict. Authors reveal the nature of characters through description, actions, and dialogue.

climax   the high point of interest in a piece of literature. The climax occurs after the conflict has been revealed, just before the action "turns" and resolution is made possible. The climax does not necessarily occur in the middle of the plot. In Guy de Maupassant's story "The Necklace," the climax occurs when Madame Loisel discovers that she has lost the necklace lent to her by Madame Forestier.

conflict   the struggle between opposing forces in a plot. The conflict provides a focus for the series of incidents that constitute the plot, arousing and holding the reader's interest. There is usually more than one conflict in a piece of literature, and a single character may experience more than one conflict. Conflict usually occurs between the main character, called the *protagonist,* and either external or internal forces.

External forces include nature, another character, and society. In "Icarus and Daedalus," Icarus' desire to fly is opposed by the sun, a force of nature. In "Growing Up," the boy Russell experiences conflict with another character, his mother. He also is in minor conflict with society when he intimates that society still believed a boy could grow up to be President, yet he has no "gumption," no desire for power.

Internal conflict occurs when a character experiences some kind of turmoil within the soul. Often this kind of conflict results from the protagonist's desire to do right versus his or her drive to achieve power or wealth at any cost. Inner conflict may also stem from the opposition of a character's fear of something and a strong desire or need to overcome this fear. In "The Road Not Taken," the narrator's inner conflict is resolved when he decides to follow the untrodden path.

dialogue   the conversation among characters in a literary work. Through dialogue an author often reveals the nature of characters.

figurative language   the use of descriptive language to make comparisons. Figurative language includes the poetic devices of simile, metaphor, and personification. Through the use of figurative language, an author may create a desired mood, calling upon the reader's imagination to make unexpected comparisons. See *simile, metaphor,* and *personification.*

flashback   a narrative device in which events told in the present are interrupted to tell about an event or events that occurred earlier. Flashbacks may be used to show how the past ties in with the present, thereby unifying the story.

foreshadowing   the hinting of something to come before it happens. Baker's statement that begins "Growing Up" is a foreshadowing of the time when he is indeed a full-fledged journalist.

hubris   excessive pride or arrogance. The ancient Greeks believed that it was hubris before the gods that caused a human's downfall.

imagery   the use of descriptive language to create pictures, or *images,* that appeal to the reader's sense of sight, touch, taste, hearing, or smell. A writer's imagery creates the tone and mood of the piece. In "It is a Beauteous Evening, Calm and Free," William Wordsworth described the evening with this image:

> . . . the broad sun
> Is sinking down in its tranquillity;
> The gentleness of heaven broods o'er the sea[.]

In "Ulysses," Tennyson described the end of day with this image:

> The lights begin to twinkle from the rocks;
> The long day wanes; the slow moon climbs; the deep
> Moans round with many voices.

metaphor   an implied analogy or comparison in which two things or qualities, usually thought of as being dissimilar, are said to be each other. A metaphor helps the reader to see something in a new way. Examples of metaphors are "The car was his chariot," and "The stars in the sky were jewels on blue velvet."

mood   the general feeling or atmosphere of a work. Mood, usually established early in a work, is conveyed by word choice, figurative language, imagery, and connotation. An author may create a mood through the description of the setting. For example, if the setting is dark and sinister, the mood is generally one of gloom.

myth   an anonymous, usually ancient, story created by people to help explain the world around them. Some myths deal with nature and the natural world, while other myths show how one should or should not behave.

nonfiction   writing based on fact rather than on imagination. Nonfiction may be based on a writer's own experience as well as on research. Nonfiction can have different purposes—to share information, to share an experience, to persuade, or to entertain. Biographies, autobiographies, personal narratives, articles, reports, essays, reference works, history books, how-to books, travel guides, and textbooks are all examples of nonfiction. Examples of nonfiction in this book include "Growing Up," the selections on mythology in Unit 4, "Lincoln's Reply," and "Early Theories of Flight."

onomatopoeia   the creation or use of words that imitate the sounds they represent. "The sausage *sizzled* in the pan," and "The *splashing* of the waves could be heard from the deck" are examples of onomatopoeia.

parable   a story that asks a question or teaches a moral or religious lesson through the use of an extended metaphor. In a parable, the principal characters and actions stand for ideas and ideals in the real world. The reader must figure out the lesson of the parable.

personification   a form of figurative language in which animals, plants, or inanimate objects are represented as having human characteristics and traits. In William Wordsworth's "Daffodils," the narrator personifies these flowers as "dancing in the breeze" and "Tossing their heads."

plot   the series of events or actions that take place in a story. During the course of the plot, events progress through rising action (in which the conflict is revealed) to the climax, or high point of tension. As the plot unravels following the climax, the story proceeds through falling action, and the resolution, or dénouement, is revealed.

point of view   the voice, or person, through whose eyes a story is told. A story may be told in the first or the third person, and a point of view may be limited or omniscient.

repetition   a technique for achieving emphasis by using sounds or words more than once as part of a pattern in a work. Repetition also gives shape to a work. In "The Road Not Taken," Frost uses this device as he repeats the opening line "Two roads diverged . . ." in the last stanza of the poem.

resolution   that part of the plot in which the solution to the conflict is revealed.

rhythm   the beat of a poem, determined usually by the pattern of stressed and unstressed syllables. Rhythm is a technical device employed by poets to support the sound and meaning of a poem.

> Jack ănd Jı́ll wĕnt úp thĕ hı́ll
> Tŏ fétch ă páil ŏf wátĕr.
> Jack fĕll dówn ănd brόke hĭs crόwn,
> Ănd Jı́ll căme túmblĭng áftĕr.

rising action the series of events in a plot that lead to the climax, or high point, of a story.

setting the place and time in which a story occurs. The details of setting often help to create the mood of a piece of literature.

simile a form of figurative language in which a comparison is made using the words *like* or *as*. In "Daffodils," William Wordsworth compares himself to a cloud as he says, "I wandered lonely *as a cloud / That floats on high o'er vales and hills . . .*"

stanza a grouping of two or more lines within a poem. Sometimes the grouping of lines within a poem is achieved by rhyme, as in "The Road Not Taken." Usually a stanza in poetry, like a paragraph in prose, deals with one main idea.

symbol the literary device of using a concrete person or object to represent something else, often an abstract idea. The dove, for example, is often used as a symbol for peace.

theme the main idea of a writing. Some themes have reappeared for centuries in a variety of cultures. In "First Time Aloft," the theme is that of initiation: the young sailor, Buttons, is initiated into adult life on the high seas. The elegy "O Captain! My Captain!" expresses the theme of sorrow and lament for someone who has died. Long works may have several themes. Some of the themes in Shakespeare's *Macbeth*, for example, are ambition and its consequences, the disruption of order in a kingdom, and the conflict between good and evil.

tone the attitude displayed by a writer toward his or her subject and audience. Vocabulary and figurative language are means of expressing tone. Some words that describe tone are *ironic, mournful, serious, amusing, formal*, and *informal*. The tone of "Growing Up" is humorous.

Evaluating Composition

The discussion of methods for teaching composition inevitably leads to the question of evaluation. How should student writing be evaluated?

There are many methods of evaluating composition. Some methods are based on a general overall impression; others evaluate papers on the basis of separate criteria. Some methods are practical with large groups; other methods are effective for individual or small group use.

Although some methods of evaluation take more time than others, evaluating student compositions *need not be a lengthy process.* The intent of this section is to describe various methods of evaluation that have been found effective in classroom practice. Although the methods described vary in time and approach, all reflect the belief that any evaluation must consider the content, organization, and purpose—as well as the correctness—of a piece of writing. The method you choose will depend on the nature of the assignment, the age and ability of your students, and the time available.

The methods described below fall into three general categories: (1) self-evaluation, (2) peer evaluation, and (3) teacher evaluation. You may select from these methods to determine grades for the composition assignments in HOUGHTON MIFFLIN ENGLISH and for other classroom assignments if you wish.

Self-evaluation

It is the philosophy of HOUGHTON MIFFLIN ENGLISH that students should be taught how to evaluate their own and one another's writing *before* teachers evaluate it.

The Writing Process lessons of HOUGHTON MIFFLIN ENGLISH provide students with three checkpoints: (1) In **revising**, students are taught to check their own work for content, organization, and clarity of language. (2) While **proofreading**, they check their papers for spelling, mechanics, and grammar errors. (3) While **preparing their final copy**, they check handwriting or typing, manuscript form, and neatness. When students are given time and instruction for doing their best *before* the teacher grades their work, they are motivated to take advantage of these checkpoints.

Teachers can, of course, offer informal evaluation at these checkpoints in the composition process but should reserve final evaluation and grading for finished papers.

Here are some suggestions for using self-evaluation techniques.

1. Have students evaluate their papers against a checklist. Checklists for each type of writing taught through the Writing Process appear in Part III (Self-evaluation Masters) and may be duplicated. Students can use the first part of the checklist at the revising stage, the second part as they do the proofreading lesson, and the third part as they make their final copies.

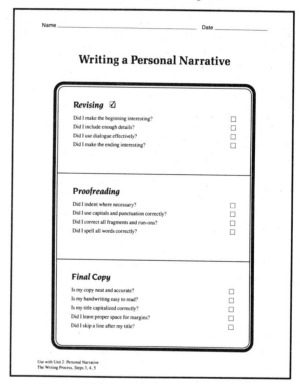

Name _____ Date _____

Writing a Personal Narrative

Revising ☑
Did I make the beginning interesting? ☐
Did I include enough details? ☐
Did I use dialogue effectively? ☐
Did I make the ending interesting? ☐

Proofreading
Did I indent where necessary? ☐
Did I use capitals and punctuation correctly? ☐
Did I correct all fragments and run-ons? ☐
Did I spell all words correctly? ☐

Final Copy
Is my copy neat and accurate? ☐
Is my handwriting easy to read? ☐
Is my title capitalized correctly? ☐
Did I leave proper space for margins? ☐
Did I skip a line after my title? ☐

Use with Unit 2: Personal Narrative
The Writing Process, Steps 3, 4, 5

If their papers satisfy an item on the checklist, students check it off. If not, they make notes that will help them improve that part of their papers. They check off the item *after* making their revisions or corrections. A separate Proofreading Checklist appears on page 51. Students can use this list for any kind of writing.

2. Use individualized checklists that focus on your students' specific writing problems. These checklists can help you pinpoint individual problems at the stage of revision, proofreading, and/or final copy. A blank form for this purpose appears on page 45 (Self-evaluation Master) and may be duplicated. A sample of a completed form showing what one student might check for appears below.

Name *Susan Glazer*   Date *September 14, 1990*

Title *Personal Narrative*

Revising
- Did I give enough information at the beginning? ☐
- Did I use interesting and varied vocabulary? ☐
- Did I vary the length of my sentences? ☐

Proofreading
- Did I punctuate quotations correctly? ☐
- Did I use commas in compound sentences? ☐

Final Copy
- Did I leave out any sentences or words? ☐
- Did I write the same word twice? ☐

Use with any kind of writing at the revising, proofreading, and publishing stages.

3. Have students rate their finished papers *before you do*, and give them the opportunity to make further changes if they find new faults. Give students copies of the rating scale you will use to evaluate their finished papers. See Part III for evaluation forms that list the skills taught in each Literature and Writing unit in HOUGHTON MIFFLIN ENGLISH, along with a range of ratings (Teacher Evaluation Masters). Have students circle the ratings they think their own papers deserve. A detailed discussion of this method of analytical evaluation appears on pages 20–22.

Peer Evaluation

The peer writing conference is usually the most vital and productive part of the writing process. Because most writing is directed to an audience, peer response provides a good opportunity for students to find out how well their compositions communicate their messages. Peer response also helps students develop the ability to recognize the strengths and weaknesses in their own writing and in the writing of others.

Sometimes using a form for response during the initial writing conference can help focus students' attention. Peer Evaluation Master A on page 46, shown below, can be duplicated for this purpose. It provides space for students to write one or two positive comments and one or two constructive suggestions for improvement as they listen to a partner read his or her draft.

Your name *Alicia Perez*   Date *September 18, 1990*

Writer's name *Susan Glazer*

✶ ✶ ✶ ✶ ✶ ✶ ✶ ✶ ✶ ✶ ✶ ✶ ✶ ✶ ✶

Write one or two things you like about this writer's paper.
1. I like the way you used dialogue to tell the story. It really made your story come alive.
2. The ending of your story was terrific. It really surprised me, and it made perfect sense.

Write one or two ideas for making the paper better.
1. I didn't understand where you were at the beginning of the story. Were you already at the park?
2. I got a little confused in the second paragraph. All of the sentences were so long.

Use for a writing conference about any kind of writing.

The following peer evaluation techniques should be used *after*, not along with, the first writing conference and the students' subsequent revision. To ensure revision and to save your time, you may want to require students to get one or two signed peer evaluations *before* they ask you to critique their papers.

1. After the revising lesson, when students have had their conferences and revised their papers, have them evaluate one another's papers against a checklist. Peer Evaluation Masters for each Writing Process assignment in this level appear in Part III and may be duplicated. These masters include the same "Revising" skills included on the Self-evaluation Masters.

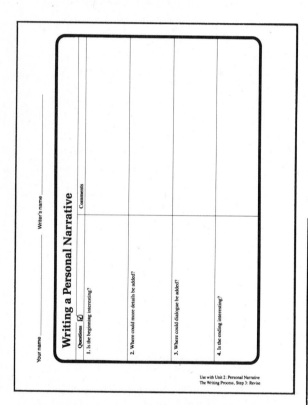

Papers can be evaluated by individual students or by students working in groups. Students should respond after *listening to,* rather than reading, each other's papers. If students divide into small groups, have each student read his or her paper aloud. After students write their comments about each paper, allow time for each writer to discuss the comments with the group.

If you use the group approach, you may wish to assign one skill to each student in the group. Each student listens for that single aspect as the

paper is read. Obviously, you will soon learn how well each of your students recognizes strengths and weaknesses in a piece of writing, and you can use this information to structure peer response groups.

2. You may want to create an individualized checklist that focuses on your class's or on an individual student's specific writing problems. This checklist, too, should be used *after* the revising lesson, can be filled out by one or more students, and should be completed after *listening to* one another's papers.

The form shown below (Peer Evaluation Master B) appears on page 47 and may be duplicated. At the top of each skill box, fill in the specific skill that you wish to have students evaluate. Have students fill in their own names and the names of the other members of the group. Each student writes his or her comments about a particular paper next to the writer's name. When finished, students cut apart their evaluation sheets and give the appropriate section to each member of the group. Students can then review the comments as they make their revisions.

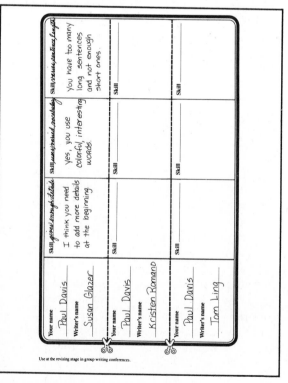

3. Have students double-check each other's papers for proofreading errors before they make their final copies. They can use check marks to identify places where corrections are needed on the revised drafts. Have students use the Proofreading Checklist on page 51.

The Teacher as Evaluator

Teacher evaluation, like students' self-evaluation and peer evaluation, can occur (1) during the composition process and/or (2) when the final copy is completed.

During the composition process your evaluation should be informal, geared toward helping students find ways to improve their writing.

Some students may benefit from your informal evaluation at the prewriting stage so that they do not spend time planning and developing a first draft for an unsuitable topic.

The first draft stage can also be a rewarding evaluation checkpoint for some students. Although you will usually want to stay out of the business of looking at students' papers until they have conferred with their peers, a quick look at a first draft will help you identify papers that are completely unfocused. A few minutes of careful questioning can usually uncover the part of the topic that most interests a student, and you may want to suggest a new first draft focusing on that topic before students go on to the revising step.

After students have had writing conferences and made their own revisions, you may want to read and discuss the papers with them individually. The revising step of the writing process is an ideal point for you to provide feedback.

Students who have difficulty identifying proofreading errors may also benefit from an informal evaluation following the proofreading step and prior to making a final copy. Similarly, some students may profit from informal reassurance about their plans for making a final copy.

For practical purposes, the formal methods of teacher evaluation have been divided into three sections, identified as general, analytic, and holistic. The one point to keep in mind, whatever method you use, is that *if evaluation is to be fair, it must be predictable*. Make sure that students know the criteria by which you will assess their papers before the final copy stage.

General Evaluation

Here are suggestions for providing appropriate general comments during the composition process or when assigning a final grade.

1. Before students prepare a final copy, use a duplicate of the form on page 48 (Teacher Evaluation Master A) to tell students what is strong about their papers and to suggest ways they could make them better. You can focus on the skills listed on the unit-by-unit Self-evaluation and Peer Evaluation Masters, or you can comment on any other characteristics of good writing that you and your students develop.

2. Use the same form to evaluate students' *finished* compositions. See whether students improved their papers in ways you suggested. If you gave a score along with your earlier comments, make sure your final score reflects the quality of the students' revision and proofreading. Tell how their final compositions are strong. Suggest what they might pay special attention to the next time they write a composition of the same type.

Student's name *Susan Glazer* Date *September 25, 1990*
Assignment *Personal Narrative* Score (Optional) _____
★ · ★ · ★ · ★ · ★ · ★ · ★ · ★ · ★ · ★ · ★ · ★ · ★ · ★ · ★

Your paper is strong in these ways:
Your use of dialogue really made your characters come alive.
Your wonderful description of the park made me feel like I was there.

Your paper could be made better in these ways:
Give more details right at the beginning about where you were.
You might want to tell how you felt when you found the notebook in the park.

Analytic Evaluation

Analytic evaluation assesses the individual elements of a piece of writing. The elements may be general, such as "content" and "organization," or they may be specific to a certain type of writing, such as "steps are in sequence" or "story beginning catches interest." Both general and specific elements can be rated on a scale.

Because analytic evaluation scales rate specific features, they are extremely useful tools for diagnosing and assessing students' writing.

- They show students how their writing is strong and what they need to improve.

- They help teachers identify the accomplishments and needs of individual students and of a class.

- They can help a school or district identify instructional objectives, structure an appropriate curriculum, and assess results.

- They enable teachers to give students a great deal of information clearly, consistently, and in far less time than other methods require.

Two types of scales serve these purposes: general analytic scales, and scales tailored to each kind of writing. Both types, and suggestions for ways to use them, are discussed in the sections that follow.

General Analytic Scales

The analytic scale on this page also appears on page 49 and may be duplicated. It lists general features that you can apply to any type of writing. This scale assigns 50 points to content, organization, and clarity of language; 30 points to grammar, capitalization and punctuation, and spelling; and 20 points to handwriting and manuscript form. You may wish to assign different weights to the categories, a simple process that is explained below. The rationale for the weights selected here is (1) that *at least* half of a student's grade should be based on the major features of any piece of writing and (2) that issues of handwriting and neatness are less important than features of mechanics and grammar.

To use the General Analytic Scale, circle the appropriate rating for each feature and add the points. The lowest score possible is 20; the highest is 100. (Note that these are *scores*, not percents.) To report a score as a letter grade or as a percent, use the Conversion Table on page 50.

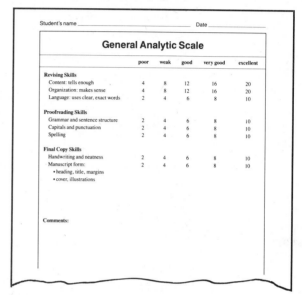

As an alternative, you can compose your own scale by adapting the General Analytic Scale shown above. Fill in the elements appropriate to the age and/or abilities of your students, and assign ratings to each element. Specific suggestions that can save you much time follow.

How to Build an Analytic Scale

1. Select elements related to revising, proofreading, and preparing a final copy.

   Revising
   - Content
   - Organization
   - Language (clarity, exactness, and color, rather than grammar or usage)

   Proofreading
   - Grammar and sentence structure
   - Punctuation and capitalization
   - Spelling

   Final Copy
   - Legibility and neatness
   - Manuscript form

2. Make sure that items are clearly worded, discrete (with little or no overlap), and essential for good writing. Choose three to four items for lower elementary, seven to eight items for junior high.

3. Distribute 100 points among the elements, with *at least* 50 for those related to content, organization, and language. Start with a maximum number that is divisible by 5 and assign five scores to each element.

4. Use the Conversion Table on page 50 to report scores as letter grades or percents.

Analytic Scales for Specific Types of Writing

Even more useful than general analytic scales are those that identify elements of specific types of writing. The form on this page shows an analytic scale for a persuasive letter. Because the elements to be checked match the skills taught in the Reading and Writing unit on the Persuasive Letter, the scale is easy for students to understand. Students are also quick to see the fairness of an evaluation that is clearly based on their textbook. (Notice that the elements to be checked are the same ones that students are asked to check on the Self-evaluation Master for the Persuasive Letter on page 151.)

In Part III you will find analytic evaluation scales for every type of writing taught in HOUGHTON MIFFLIN ENGLISH (Teacher Evaluation Masters). The elements to be checked on each scale match the skills that students practice in lessons for revising, proofreading, and preparing their final copy of each type. You may duplicate these forms, or you may compose your own analytic scale for a type of writing, using the General Analytic Scale on page 49 as a guide.

Ways to Use Analytic Evaluation

Here are suggestions for ways to use analytic evaluation scales.

1. Have students rate their own or others' compositions on an analytic scale. Compare your ratings with theirs. Discuss any differences.

Student's name _____ Date _____

Persuasive Letter: Analytic Scale

	poor	weak	good	very good	excellent
Revising Skills					
Opinion stated clearly	—	—	—	—	—
Reasons and facts support opinion	—	—	—	—	—
Reasons ordered effectively	—	—	—	—	—
Topic sentence for each paragraph	—	—	—	—	—
Purpose is clear	—	—	—	—	—
Persuasive strategies used	—	—	—	—	—
Proofreading Skills					
Proper business letter form	—	—	—	—	—
Capitals used correctly	—	—	—	—	—
Punctuation used correctly	—	—	—	—	—
Abbreviations and numbers used correctly	—	—	—	—	—
Words spelled correctly	—	—	—	—	—
Final Copy Skills					
Neat and accurate	—	—	—	—	—
Easy to read	—	—	—	—	—
Title capitalized correctly	—	—	—	—	—
Margins properly spaced	—	—	—	—	—
Title followed by line of space	—	—	—	—	—

Comments:

Total score _____

Letter grade or percent _____

Use with Unit 10: Persuasive Letter
The Writing Process, Steps 3, 4, 5

2. Compare "first try" scores with later scores on writing of a particular type.

3. Compare scores on students' writing at the beginning of the year with scores on the same type of writing, obtained under the same circumstances, at the end of the year.

4. If you are teaching several subjects in a classroom, use an analytic scale to grade writing assignments in other subjects. Phrase the assignment carefully so that you can assign weights to each of its key elements. *Before they write,* students should know each element you will be assessing. Give at least half of the total points for elements related to content, organization, and clarity of language. Be sure to divide the score for each item into five ratings, and be sure the maximum score is 100 so that you can use the same Conversion Table for all writing. (If you want to give more weight to some assignments than to others, simply count the final grade for a given assignment two or three times when you

average grades for a marking period.) The analytic scale below is based on the following science-class assignment: *Write one paragraph that clearly explains how to make a cultured pearl. Put the steps in the process in chronological order. Use transitional words to indicate the beginning of each step. End your explanation with a sentence that reaches a definite conclusion.*

EVALUATION SCALE

Content, organization, clarity of language

Includes all steps	6 12 18 24 30
Explains steps clearly	6 12 18 24 30
Steps are in order	2 4 6 8 10
Uses transitional words	1 2 3 4 5
Has a good ending	1 2 3 4 5

Grammar, sentence structure*	2 4 6 8 10
Punctuation, spelling*	1 2 3 4 5
Heading, legibility, margins*	1 2 3 4 5

*When students have no chance to revise and proofread, these weights should be low.

5. Use analytic scales to prepare students for proficiency tests or writing assessments, including those that will be scored holistically.

Focused Holistic Evaluation

Holistic evaluation is based on the idea that the elements of a composition work together to achieve communication of information and ideas. Thus, when you evaluate a composition, you assign a single score to reflect how successfully the writer has handled the elements of content, organization, language, punctuation, and other conventions.

A variety of holistic evaluation techniques have been developed to suit different needs and situations. In proficiency testing, papers are frequently scored by comparison to sample papers that represent the range of possible scores, such as 0–4. These sample papers are acquired by administering the test to a small group of representative students prior to general testing or by selecting representative samples after the test has been administered to the entire group. The expected features of papers that would fall into each scoring category are identified on the basis of these sample papers and listed in a scoring guide.

The method known as focused holistic scoring is appropriate for both large-scale proficiency testing and classroom evaluation. Like other holistic techniques, focused holistic scoring evaluates the composition as a whole and scores papers using a scoring guide. However, this method focuses on a student's ability to write for a specific purpose. The purpose may be to give instructions, to describe, to relate a personal narrative, to convey factual information in a report, to convey thoughts or information in a letter, to persuade, or to convey information gained in an interview, among others. (The terms *informative*, *expressive*, and *persuasive* are sometimes used to describe purposes.) General criteria are developed before the writing assignment is prepared— rather than after, as in other forms of holistic evaluation— and are refined after the assignment is written.

The Assignment

The writing assignment for holistic evaluation usually consists of a picture stimulus and written directions for writing about the picture. The writing assignment should state the type of writing to be done, such as a description or a personal narrative. In a testing situation, the specific topic should also be given and it must be one that all students can relate to and write about. The assignment should also provide cues to the characteristics of successful papers. The sample assignment on page 25 is clearly related to its scoring guide.

If you are using the holistic technique in the classroom to evaluate student compositions, you do not need to assign the same topic to all students. For classroom writing, it is usually better to have students select their own topics.

The Scoring Guide

Each writing assignment is accompanied by an explanation and a scoring guide. The scoring guide describes the criteria for each possible score. The criteria are based on (1) the kind of writing being evaluated, such as descriptions or stories; (2) the information given in the assignment; (3) the students' ages and abilities; (4) the audience; and (5) the nature of the writing situation. Each of these is discussed below.

In considering *the kind of writing*, the criteria might specify that logical order and clearly presented facts should be part of a well-written research report or that a plot with a conflict, a climax, and a resolution should be an important element of a story.

The *assignment itself* will contain specific elements that the composition should include and that the criteria must consider. For example, an assignment that asks students to give instructions on how to make a bird feeder might specify that all the items shown in the picture stimulus be included in the description.

The criteria also take into consideration *the students' ages and abilities*. Long stringy sentences are common in papers written by third and fourth grade students, but this style would not be as acceptable in the writing of a junior high student. There may also be a greater tolerance of spelling and mechanical errors at early levels, particularly if students are attempting to use a rich vocabulary for their level.

If an *audience* is designated for the assignment, the criteria will consider whether or not the composition is appropriate for that audience.

Finally, the criteria must consider the *nature of the writing situation*. In a testing situation, students have little opportunity for prewriting activities and limited time for writing. In addition, they may not be able to use reference sources. In these situations, the scoring criteria should be more lenient toward certain stylistic and mechanical errors. If the composition is produced following a series of steps that include revising and proofreading, as in the HOUGHTON MIFFLIN ENGLISH composition units, the criteria for such errors might be more stringent.

How effectively a student integrates all these elements and considerations to communicate a message determines a paper's overall score.

Scoring

In a testing situation, papers are evaluated by a team of two readers who understand and agree on the criteria beforehand. A third person, who also understands and agrees on the criteria, must be available to read those papers that receive two different scores.

The actual evaluation of compositions should be a *quick* process. Readers should respond to their first overall impression of the paper and score it accordingly. Counting of any sort, such as the number of spelling errors or the number of order words, is *not* a part of the holistic scoring method.

In the classroom, teachers may want to work together in teams when using holistic evaluation. In preparing a scoring guide, you may want to predetermine general criteria based on composition skills students have been taught, then refine the criteria, using representative class papers that were written in response to the assignment.

A model of a holistically scored assignment appears on the following pages.

A Model for Holistic Scoring

In this section you will find a model of a holistically scored assignment. The section includes a sample writing assignment, a model scoring guide for the assignment, and sample scored papers with accompanying explanations. This model represents the use of holistic scoring in a testing situation in which students may not have an opportunity to proofread.

Writing Prompt: A Description

Directions: This picture shows an animal called an aardvark. An aardvark lives in underground burrows. It eats ants and termites, which it digs for in the ground. Write a paragraph that describes how an aardvark looks. Describe an aardvark so clearly that classmates who have never seen an aardvark will be able to picture one in their minds after reading your description.

Remember to:
- choose details that help create the overall impression that you want to give
- use exact nouns, verbs, adjectives, and adverbs that create a clear mental picture
- use descriptive language that makes comparisons
- organize your details in a way that makes sense

Explanation

Students are to write a descriptive paragraph about the appearance of an aardvark, using the picture as a guide. The illustration and the directions provide all of the information that students need to complete the assignment.

The aardvark was selected as the subject of the assignment because of its prominent and unusual features. The short feet, long ears, small eyes, pig-like snout and body, and long pointed tail are unusual and dramatic in combination. Students should be able to describe these features easily because they

are so evident. In addition, the directions draw attention to the aardvark's sharp claws.

Students should use exact words to create a vivid mental image. Some students might compare or contrast the aardvark or parts of its body to other animals or objects. Students should show an awareness of the audience by choosing comparisons familiar to most students their age. In addition, the paragraph should be well organized so that the description develops logically and smoothly.

The directions specify that students describe only the aardvark's appearance. They are not asked to tell about the animal's habits or where it lives or to give any other information. If knowledgeable students include additional facts about the aardvark, they should do so in a way that contributes to, rather than interrupts, the description.

Scoring Guide

The following sample scoring guide accompanies this assignment. The guide describes five possible scores and lists features of representative papers in each category. This model is only one example of a scoring guide that might be used with the given assignment.

0 – Papers in this category do not respond to the assignment. Examples:
- an illegible paper
- a paper about a different topic
- a paper that simply restates or comments on the assignment

1 – Papers in this category deal abruptly or indirectly with the assignment. Examples:
- a story, rather than a descriptive paragraph, about an aardvark
- an informative paragraph that describes how the aardvark obtains food rather than what the animal looks like
- a descriptive paragraph that attempts to tell what the animal looks like but does so in a very confused, nearly unintelligible way
- a descriptive paragraph that includes only one or two brief, general statements about the aardvark's appearance

2 – Papers in this category respond to the assignment in a sketchy or inconsistent way. Examples:
- a paragraph that describes the aardvark clearly but in a random, disorganized way
- a paragraph that describes the aardvark completely but in a very general way
- a paragraph that provides a detailed partial description but then digresses

3 – Papers in this category give a complete description of an aardvark. A number of details allow the reader to obtain a clear picture of the animal. The paragraphs are generally well organized and read logically. Examples:
- a paragraph that meets the criteria of the highest category but includes nonessential information
- a paragraph that is clear and well structured but needs additional details or more exact vocabulary to make the description vivid
- a paragraph that is fully detailed and well organized but has so many mechanical or spelling errors that it is difficult to read
- a well-written paragraph that makes comparisons that are too abstract or unfamiliar to the audience

4 – Papers in this category are unified, well organized, and explicitly detailed so that the reader can easily visualize an aardvark. Papers in this category include all the strong points of papers in the 3 category, but they are more skillfully and consistently presented. Some features of these paragraphs:
- accurate, exact vocabulary that creates a vivid mental image
- accurate, familiar comparisons that clarify specific features
- a logical, smooth presentation

Sample Papers

The following samples represent scoring categories 1–4. Each paper is followed by a brief explanation of its score. Titles have been provided.

The Aardvark

Ted and me were walking threw the jungle and we herd a funny noise and suddenly there was this funny creature running around and snorting and digging up the ground. Ted said "What is that"? I said. "It looks like a giant pig or something. We had better be careful. it might be dangerous. We took a picture of it. then the animal saw us and looked very mad so we took off. When we got back to our camp. we looked it up in an animal book and found out that it is an ardvaark.

Score: 1

Explanation: The writer wrote a story instead of a descriptive paragraph.

> ### The Aardvark
>
> The Ardvark is a strange animal. I always thought an Ardvark was a bird. What a surprise to find out that it looks sort of like a pig! It has a big nose like a pigs and tall ears. I bet it can hear real well because rabbits have tall ears and they hear real well. It's not as big as a bush, and it has a long tail. I would like to have an Ardvark to keep and I'd take it for walks on a leash.

Score: 2

Explanation: The writer describes the aardvark in general terms. The general reference to a pig implies that the entire animal, rather than just parts of it, looks like a pig. The writer also includes personal thoughts and opinions that interrupt and detract from the description.

> ### The Aardvark
>
> I've never seen anything as ugly and stange as an aardvark. It makes me think of my Uncle's dog Red. It's real ugly. Anyway an aardvark has a snout that looks like a pig's and it has tiny eyes that look like pig's eyes, too. It's ears are longer than a pig's though, and stand up straight on its head. It has a hump in its back and short legs. Its toes look very sharp. It's not very tall-- just about the size of a bush. It has a long ugly tail that narrows to a point. I hope I never have to see a real one.

Score: 3

Explanation: This paper fulfills the purpose of the assignment. The writer describes each of the aardvark's major features more or less accurately and in a logical order. Some vocabulary, however, is not as exact as it could be. For example, the writer describes the aardvark's toes, rather than claws, as sharp. In addition, the comparison with the writer's uncle's dog is not useful. The slight inaccuracies in vocabulary do not interfere with the reader's overall understanding of the aardvark's appearance.

The Aardvark

An aardvark looks like it was put together from pieces of different animal jigsaw puzzles. When you first look at it, you think it is a kind of pig because it has a snout like a pig's except that the aardvark's snout is longer. It also has small eyes like a pig's and is just a little taller and thinner than a pig.

The rest of the aardvark is not like a pig at all. It has long, pointed ears that stand up straight on its head like a donkey's ears. It has a curved back and four short legs. There are sharp claws on its feet that help it dig up the ants and termites that it eats. The long tail reminds me of a possum's tail because it is thick near the body and narrow and pointed at the tip. The aardvark is truly a very unusual animal.

Score: 4

Explanation: This paper is unified, smooth, and fully detailed. The writer describes the aardvark in detail, using exact words and comparisons. The paragraph begins with a sentence that states the main idea; it provides supporting details and ends with a summary statement.

How to Get Ready for a Proficiency Test

To perform well on a test, students need to be familiar with the form of the test, the testing conditions, and how the test will be scored. Here are suggestions for preparing your students to take a writing proficiency test that will be evaluated by holistic scoring.

1. Show students a sample test or an actual test from previous years, or use the test on page 24 in A Model for Holistic Scoring. (The test included in this model is one of the most common forms used by states and school districts.)

   Point out these features of the test:
   - *type* of writing to be done (instructions, description, narration, persuasion, etc.)
   - *cues* in the test question/assignment for content, organization, language, and audience
   - *criteria* for awarding the highest holistic score
   - *fit* between cues in the test assignment and criteria in the scoring guide*

2. Work through a sample test with the whole class. If you wish, you may use one of the Writing Prompts in Part III.

3. Discuss sample papers with your class. You may duplicate the four sample papers on pages 25–27. Have students point out the weaknesses and strengths of the papers. To make the distinctions among poor, good, and excellent papers clear, you may want to begin with the score 1 sample, jump to the score 3 sample, and end with the score 4 sample.

4. Conduct a "For Free!" test day as a trial run. Assign the type of writing and give the directions that students will be given on the "real" test day. If test conditions will not permit revising and proofreading, advise students to spend most of their time on the elements that will count most when papers are scored. For practice, you may use any of the Writing Prompts in Part III. These assignments cover the types of writing that are most frequently tested—and they match the types of writing taught in the Literature and Writing units of HOUGHTON MIFFLIN ENGLISH. Two sets of assignments, labeled I and II, are given for each type. If you use a Writing Prompt I assignment for practice, you can use the Writing Prompt II assignment for further practice and/or for purposes of comparison with scores on the first assignment.

5. To show students what they must do to score well, create an analytic scale showing the criteria for a paper. Score the practice papers with a holistic score of 4.

   If you want to compose your own assignment and your own scale, see How to Build an Analytic Scale on pages 20–21. To convert scores into letter grades or percents, see the Conversion Table on page 50.

6. Discuss the scores on sample papers with students. Teach or reteach lessons that will help them make the greatest gains.

7. Ask students to discuss strategies for writing well. Ask them to tell what to do if they feel nervous or if they "get stuck." Have them compose a list of "do's" and "don'ts" to remember on test day. Post their ideas.

---

*These should match, but sometimes test assignments that teachers are required to use are so general that students are left to guess what they should include, how they should organize their writing, or how they should choose language appropriate to an audience. In these unfortunate circumstances, you could tell students that they need to remember what they have been taught in HOUGHTON MIFFLIN ENGLISH Writing Process lessons about content, organization, and clarity of language for the type of writing on the test.

Oral Language Checklist

These lists of listening and speaking skills provide you with a road map to evaluate your students' needs and progress in selected skill areas. Side 1 allows you to measure an individual's performance in writing conferences, class discussions, and instructions. Side 2 is intended to be distributed. It is a checklist that both you and your students can use in judging a speaker's performance.

Interest Inventory

Use this at the beginning of the year. You may want students to hand in their Inventories to you as a way of getting acquainted. Be sure, however, that students get their Inventories back *before they begin to write.* These Inventories should be the first items to go into students' writing folders. They are an excellent prewriting resource. Students will find in them germs of ideas for each type of writing taught in the Writing Process lessons in their Student Books.

Ideas for Sharing Books

This resource suggests a variety of creative ideas for presenting books, whether the reading has been assigned or free. For some students, you may wish to duplicate the list and allow them to choose ideas on their own. For other students, either assign an idea appropriate to a book the student has read, or provide four or five ideas and allow the student to choose one.

Book Report Masters

Both the Student Book and this *Teacher's Resources* book contain a rich assortment of suggestions for students to draw on as they share and report on their reading. However, there may be times when you want to introduce a short and simple form that students can use independently to keep you abreast of their reading. Several simple book report forms for various kinds of books appear in this section for you to duplicate as appropriate.

(continued)

Writing Evaluation Masters

These Masters are generic forms for evaluating any kind of writing. Masters for specific types of writing are provided in each Literature and Writing unit in Part III.

The **Self-evaluation Master** allows you to write in skills that need to be emphasized (1) in your particular classroom or (2) for a particular student whose needs may be different from those of the rest of the class.

Peer Evaluation Master A can be used during the writing conference by pairs or groups of students. Ask students to be *specific* in their ideas for making the papers better.

Peer Evaluation Master B is for use in group conferences, preferably after the initial writing conference. You, the teacher, should write the points you want the group to evaluate in the short skill lines in the boxes. Group members should then listen for the three areas you have pinpointed and make notes as they listen or during the discussion afterward.

Teacher Evaluation Master A is a general evaluation form. It provides space for positive comments and suggestions for improvement. It could be especially useful *during* the revising stage, as well as for post-revision evaluation.

Teacher Evaluation Master B is a General Analytic Scale. It provides general characteristics of good, correct writing that can be used for any kind of writing assignment. A numerical scale is also provided.

The **Conversion Table** gives you a convenient formula to report scores as letter grades or percents.

Proofreading Checklist and Proofreading Marks

You will probably want to make a copy of each of these forms for students to keep in the front of their writing folders. These forms can be used for any kind of writing in any subject area.

Test-taking Strategies

Here are four lessons for you to duplicate and teach in whole-class sessions or use with individual students. Each lesson suggests strategies for approaching a specific type of standardized test question and provides practice. An Answer Key is provided at the end of the tests.

Student _____

To the teacher: You may wish to use the following checklist to evaluate student listening and speaking skills.

Oral Language Checklist

Writing Conference

	succeeds	needs improvement

Listener

	succeeds	needs improvement
listens carefully, keeps TRACK	☐	☐
starts by saying something positive	☐	☐
tells something he/she liked about the writing or accurately restates the main points	☐	☐
asks questions to clarify meaning or get more information	☐	☐
offers suggestions only when asked by the writer	☐	☐
is polite	☐	☐

Speaker

explains points listener does not understand	☐	☐
considers adding information that is needed	☐	☐
considers taking out unnecessary information	☐	☐
is polite	☐	☐

Class Discussion

Listener

is prepared; understands the topic and purpose of the discussion	☐	☐
listens carefully; keeps TRACK	☐	☐

Speaker

takes an active part	☐	☐
cooperates with the leader or chairperson	☐	☐
keeps statements brief and to the point	☐	☐
is polite, even when disagreeing with someone	☐	☐
asks thoughtful questions	☐	☐
sticks to the subject under discussion	☐	☐
gives good reasons to support his/her opinions	☐	☐
tries to get opinions from everybody	☐	☐

Instructions

Listener

listens attentively; keeps TRACK	☐	☐
asks questions if instructions or order is unclear	☐	☐

Speaker

uses content and language appropriate to purpose and audience	☐	☐
includes all necessary information	☐	☐
explains steps in order	☐	☐
uses order words (*first, next, then,* etc.)	☐	☐

Student _____

Oral Language Checklist

Student Speech

	succeeds	needs improvement
Content		
chooses a familiar or well-researched subject	☐	☐
chooses a subject that will interest both the speaker and the audience	☐	☐
prepares a speech with an interesting beginning and end	☐	☐
prepares a speech that has a point to it	☐	☐
makes purpose and subject of the speech clear	☐	☐
supplies details and examples to illustrate points made	☐	☐
includes enough information to achieve the purpose	☐	☐
uses pictures whenever appropriate	☐	☐
Delivery		
appears to have planned and rehearsed well	☐	☐
catches attention of the audience at the beginning	☐	☐
answers the questions *who? what? where? when?* and *why?*	☐	☐
puts events in correct sequence	☐	☐
speaks from memory or glances at note cards	☐	☐
shows enthusiasm for the subject	☐	☐
stands straight but not stiff; does not move around unnecessarily	☐	☐
makes eye contact with the audience; smiles	☐	☐
uses formal or informal language appropriate for the audience	☐	☐
keeps to the topic	☐	☐
speaks slowly, clearly, and loudly enough to be heard	☐	☐
varies pitch effectively by raising and lowering voice	☐	☐
uses stress for emphasis	☐	☐
varies volume, speaking loudly or softly to make important points	☐	☐
varies rate of speaking	☐	☐
pauses to emphasize important points	☐	☐
gestures to capture attention and emphasize important points	☐	☐
delivers ending the audience will remember	☐	☐

Name _____

Interest Inventory

What you know about and what you're interested in may surprise you. Fill out these pages to find out more about yourself.

1. My favorite type of movie is _____

2. My favorite kind of music is _____

3. My favorite singers are _____

4. My favorite type of TV show is _____

5. My favorite school subjects are _____

   _____

6. My greatest talent is _____

7. My favorite book is _____

8. The character in the book who interests me most is _____

   because _____

9. My favorite outdoor activity is _____

10. My favorite indoor activity is _____

11. My favorite foods are _____

12. On weekend afternoons, I'm likely to be found _____

    _____

13. The country I would most like to visit is _____

14. The person (alive or dead) I would most like to meet is _____

15. Three changes in the world that I would like to make one day are _____

    _____

    _____

16. If I could travel back in time, I would live in _____

17. When I'm older, I would like to work as a _____

18. If I could be a famous person for a day, I'd like to be _____

19. If I could be anywhere in the world now, I would be _____

33

20. If I had a million dollars, I would _____

_____

21. If I could have any wish in the world, I would wish _____

_____

_____

Check the box that best describes your interest. If you prefer a similar topic, write it in the blank space provided.

Interest Inventory

	none	know about	want to know more about
skiing	☐	☐	☐
(or _____)			
cooking	☐	☐	☐
(or _____)			
playing flute	☐	☐	☐
(or _____)			
space travel	☐	☐	☐
(or _____)			
photography	☐	☐	☐
(or _____)			
Disneyland	☐	☐	☐
(or _____)			
computers	☐	☐	☐
(or _____)			
stamps	☐	☐	☐
(or _____)			
Australia	☐	☐	☐
(or _____)			
gardening	☐	☐	☐
(or _____)			
earthquakes	☐	☐	☐
(or _____)			
dog training	☐	☐	☐
(or _____)			

camping □ □ □

(or _____)

acting □ □ □

(or _____)

dolphins □ □ □

(or _____)

Bill of Rights □ □ □

(or _____)

drawing □ □ □

(or _____)

popular music □ □ □

(or _____)

clothing □ □ □

(or _____)

dreams □ □ □

(or _____)

Which things on this list have you read in the last two years? Check them off.

_____ mysteries _____ romances _____ fan magazines

_____ sports magazines _____ history books _____ travel books

_____ detective novels _____ how-to books _____ science fiction

_____ news magazines _____ poetry _____ science magazines

_____ biographies _____ horror stories _____ autobiographies

_____ animal stories _____ plays _____ computer magazines

_____ newspapers _____ short stories _____ teen magazines

_____ comic books (other _____) (other _____)

Sometimes I wish I could

have X-ray vision _____

be a famous artist _____

travel in space _____

make everyone happy _____

live for a thousand years _____

be the President _____

live atop a skyscraper _____

cure all sickness _____

fly like a bird _____

travel in time _____

win a great award _____

make a great invention _____

other _____

_____

Ideas for Sharing Books

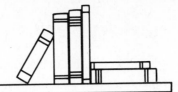

- In two or three words or brief sentences, summarize the main character of your book to your class. Then describe three or four specific scenes that show what your character is like.

- If the setting of your book is particularly vivid and important to the story, make a detailed colored drawing of it. Write a title for your drawing, using words or lines from the book.

- Make a diagram of the plot of your book, like the one on page 214 of your textbook. Include the conflict, the climax, and the resolution.

- Retell the climax without giving the ending of your book away.

- If your book contains an important symbol, make a picture or a three-dimensional representation of the symbol to show to your classmates. Explain why the symbol is important to the story.

- Choose one scene that is representative of the plot of your book. Read the scene out loud and show its relation to the entire book.

- Make a time line to show where the characters or the events in your book fit in history.

- Write a report on the life of the author of your book. Then read at least one chapter of another book by the same author. Present your report about your author's life and works to your classmates.

- If your book is a biography or an autobiography, research the family tree of the person the book is about. Ask your librarian to help you. Draw a family tree to show to your classmates. Include the person's ancestors, brothers and sisters, and descendants.

- Sometimes when we read, we feel so close to a particular character that we identify with him or her. Do you identify with a character in your book? Tell your classmates about how and why, comparing events from the book with events in your own life.

- Make one scene of your book into a musical. Choose one or two of your favorite popular songs and rewrite the lyrics to fit your book. You may even want to include dancing in your play!

- Give your classmates a sales pitch to persuade them to read your favorite book. Talk about the setting, plot, and characters of your book as well as about the author.

- Imagine that your book is being made into a movie. Choose movie stars from yesterday and today to play the main characters. Tell your classmates about your cast, explaining why you have chosen particular actors and actresses to play the characters.

Ideas for Sharing Books

- Find a famous saying that could be an inscription for all or part of your book. Tell it to your classmates, giving three specific reasons that show how the quotation illustrates your book.

- Turn an exciting scene from your book into a TV movie. Be the narrator, describing the setting and background information for your audience. Ask classmates to act out the scene under your direction. You may even want to include commercials!

- Compare and contrast a biography with an autobiography of the same person. Find an important event that is described in each book. Read these sections from both books out loud to your classmates. How are the two books alike and different? Discuss the similarities and differences, including points of view, with your classmates.

- Is there a line, a scene, or a symbol that is repeated in your book? If so, make a diagram of the main events in your story, showing where this repetition occurs. Explain to your classmates the effect of the repetition on the story.

- Give a bookstore autograph party with your class. Dress as the main character of your book, and have copies of a photo or drawing of yourself to sign and give out to fans. Answer the questions that your classmates, as fans, ask you.

- With a friend, present a TV talk show to your class. In a discussion, compare and contrast each of your views of the same book or of similar books.

- Study the opening paragraph or page of your book. Decide how it sets the stage for the rest of the book. Read the paragraph or page out loud to your class, pointing out all the important words that tell about the setting, characters, and theme of your book.

- Talk to your class about the author's tone. Is his or her attitude serious or funny? happy or sad? Give examples of the author's language and of particular events in your story that show the author's tone.

- Read two articles that have been written about your book or about its topic. Present a summary of the articles to your class. Explain how the information in the articles added to your appreciation of the book.

- How would the characters in your book and in classmates' books react in a new and different situation? Get together with a group of classmates and pretend to be the main character in each of your books. Imagine that you are all the survivors of an earthquake. What is most important to you in your lives? What are your goals? Why did you want to survive? Role-play your characters, answering these questions.

Houghton Mifflin English 8. Copyright © Houghton Mifflin Company. All rights reserved.

Name _____ Date _____

Book Report

Title _____

Author _____

Introduction _____

_____

_____

_____

Body _____

_____

_____

_____

_____

_____

_____

_____

_____

_____

Conclusion _____

_____

_____

_____

_____

_____

Book Report

Use with the Extending Literature lesson on page 84 of the Student Book.

Book Report

Book Report: Novel

Title _____

Author _____

Introduction *(Begin with an attention-getting statement or question.)*

_____

_____

_____

_____

Characters, Setting, Plot *(Tell* who, where, when, *and* what, *but don't reveal the resolution.)*

_____

_____

_____

_____

_____

_____

_____

_____

_____

_____

My opinion and recommendation _____

_____

_____

_____

Book Report: Biography

Title _____

Author _____

Introduction *(Name the subject, beginning with an attention-getting statement or question.)*

_____

_____

_____

_____

Summary *(Tell why the person is well known. Then give highlights of his or her life.)*

_____

_____

_____

_____

_____

_____

_____

_____

_____

Conclusion *(Give your opinion and recommendation.)* _____

_____

_____

_____

Book Report

Name _____ Date _____

Book Report: Autobiography

Title _____

Author _____

Introduction *(Name the subject, beginning with an attention-getting statement or question.)*

_____

_____

_____

Summary *(Tell why the person is well known. Then give highlights of his or her life.)*

_____

_____

_____

_____

_____

_____

_____

_____

Conclusion *(Did you enjoy the author's account of his or her life? Give your opinion of the book.)*

_____

_____

_____

_____

_____

_____

Name _____ Date _____

Book Report: Nonfiction

Title _____

Author _____

Introduction *(Name the topic, beginning with an attention-getting statement or question.)*

_____

_____

_____

_____

Summary *(Give some interesting facts or events.)* _____

_____

_____

_____

_____

_____

_____

_____

_____

_____

_____

Conclusion *(Give your opinion of the book and recommendation for others.)* _____

_____

_____

_____

Book Report

Name _____ Date _____

Title _____

Writing Evaluation Master

Revising

_____ ☐
_____ ☐
_____ ☐
_____ ☐
_____ ☐

Proofreading

_____ ☐
_____ ☐
_____ ☐
_____ ☐
_____ ☐

Final Copy

_____ ☐
_____ ☐
_____ ☐
_____ ☐
_____ ☐

Use with any kind of writing at the revising, proofreading, and publishing stages.

Your name _____ Date _____

Writer's name _____

★ · ★ · ★ · ★ · ★ · ★ · ★ · ★ · ★ · ★ · ★ · ★ · ★ · ★

Write one or two things you like about this writer's paper.

1. _____

_____

_____

_____

2. _____

_____

_____

_____

Write one or two ideas for making the paper better.

1. _____

_____

_____

_____

2. _____

_____

_____

_____

_____

Use for a writing conference about any kind of writing.

Writing Evaluation Master

Writing Evaluation Master

Skill _____

Skill _____

Skill _____

Skill _____

Skill _____

Skill _____

Your name _____

Writer's name _____

Your name _____

Writer's name _____

Your name _____

Writer's name _____

Use at the revising stage in group writing conferences.

TEACHER EVALUATION MASTER A

Writing Evaluation Master

Student's name _____ Date _____

Assignment _____ Score (Optional) _____

★ · ★ · ★ · ★ · ★ · ★ · ★ · ★ · ★ · ★ · ★ · ★ · ★ · ★

Your paper is strong in these ways:

_____

_____

_____

_____

Your paper could be made better in these ways:

_____

_____

_____

_____

- ✂

Student's name _____ Date _____

Assignment _____ Score (Optional) _____

★ · ★ · ★ · ★ · ★ · ★ · ★ · ★ · ★ · ★ · ★ · ★ · ★ · ★

Your paper is strong in these ways:

_____

_____

_____

_____

Your paper could be made better in these ways:

_____

_____

_____

_____

Use to evaluate any type of writing.

Student's name _____ Date _____

General Analytic Scale

	poor	weak	good	very good	excellent
Revising Skills					
Content: tells enough	4	8	12	16	20
Organization: makes sense	4	8	12	16	20
Language: uses clear, exact words	2	4	6	8	10
Proofreading Skills					
Grammar and sentence structure	2	4	6	8	10
Capitals and punctuation	2	4	6	8	10
Spelling	2	4	6	8	10
Final Copy Skills					
Handwriting and neatness	2	4	6	8	10
Manuscript form:	2	4	6	8	10
• heading, title, margins					
• cover, illustrations					

Comments:

Total score _____

Letter grade
or percent _____

Writing Evaluation Master

The Conversion Table on the next page will help you with scoring.
Use with all types of writing.

Conversion Table

Scores	Letter Grade	Percent*
97–100	A+	_____
94–96	A	_____
90–93	A–	_____
83–89	B+	_____
77–82	B	_____
70–76	B–	_____
63-69	C+	_____
57–62	C	_____
50–56	C–	_____
43–49	D+	_____
37–42	D	_____
30–36	D–	_____
20–29	F	_____

*After you use the table to determine the letter grade, you can use your own school's system for reporting the percent that matches the letter grade.

Proofreading Checklist

Does your paper have mistakes that might make it difficult to read and understand? Use the questions below to check your paper. Read each question; then correct any mistakes that you find in your paper. After you have corrected the mistakes, put a check mark in the box next to the question.

- ☐ **1.** Did I spell all words correctly?
- ☐ **2.** Did I indent correctly?
- ☐ **3.** Did I correct all fragments and run-ons?
- ☐ **4.** Did I use capital letters correctly?
- ☐ **5.** Did I end each sentence with the correct punctuation mark?
- ☐ **6.** Did I use commas, apostrophes, quotation marks, underlining, hyphens, dashes, parentheses, colons, and semicolons correctly?
- ☐ **7.** Did I use abbreviations and numbers correctly?
- ☐ **8.** Did I use the correct forms of nouns and pronouns?
- ☐ **9.** Did I use verbs and verb forms correctly?
- ☐ **10.** Did I use modifiers correctly?

Are there any special problems you should be careful of? Make your own proof-reading checklist.

- ☐ _____
- ☐ _____
- ☐ _____
- ☐ _____
- ☐ _____
- ☐ _____

Use for proofreading any kind of writing.

Proofreading Marks

Mark	Explanation	Example
¶	Begin a new paragraph. Indent the paragraph.	¶ The space shuttle landed safely after its five-day voyage. It glided to a smooth, perfect halt.
∧	Add letters, words, or sentences.	People are lively are said to have charisma.
∧ (with comma)	Add a comma.	Carlton my Siamese cat has a mind of his own.
∨ ∨	Add quotation marks.	Where do you want us to put the piano? asked the gasping movers.
⊙	Add a period.	Don't forget to put a period at the end of every statement
ℓ	Take out words, sentences, and punctuation marks. Correct spelling.	She likes movies more better than plays.
/	Change a capital letter to a small letter.	We are studying about the Louisiana Purchase in History class.
≡	Change a small letter to a capital letter.	The Nile river in africa is the longest river in the world.
∽	Reverse letters or words.	To complete the task successfully, you must follow carefully the steps.

1 Analogies

Some test items require you to complete analogies. Look at the sample.

SAMPLE: Choose the word that correctly completes the analogy. Mark your answer.

ballet : dance : : opera : _____

○ **a.** singer ○ **b.** concerto ○ **c.** waltz ○ **d.** polka ○ **e.** music

---

Strategy

1. The first step in completing an analogy is to figure out the relationship between the first two words. Some common types of relationships are part to whole, category to member, object to characteristic, object to use, worker to tool, worker to product, synonyms, and antonyms. (The first six types of relationships may be reversed, for example, whole to part.)

2. The next step is to look at the first word in the second pair. Then complete the analogy, trying each of the five answers in the blank. Each answer choice is probably related in some way to one or more words in the analogy. You must determine, however, which *one* word creates the same relationship in the second pair as the relationship you identified in the first pair.

3. Double-check your answer. Say the completed analogy to yourself, substituting for the colons the words that explain the relationship. For example, in the analogy *enemy : friend : : foe : pal*, you could substitute like this: Enemy *is an antonym for* friend *as* foe *is an antonym for* pal.

Now look at the sample again. The relationship between ballet and dance is member to category—in other words, ballet is a form of dance. What answer choice names a category of which opera is a member? Answer **a,** *singer,* is related to opera but is not a category. Answer **b,** *concerto,* is another member, or form of music. Answers **c** and **d,** *polka* and *waltz,* are both other forms of dance and would not be a category for opera. Each of the choices is related to music or dance, but only music is the category into which opera can fit. The correct answer is **e.**

Practice: Analogies

Choose the word that correctly completes each analogy. Mark your answer.

1. birch : tree : : petunia : _____
- ○ **a.** petal
- ○ **b.** pretty
- ○ **c.** flower
- ○ **d.** garden
- ○ **e.** rose

2. money : wallet : : wrench : _____
- ○ **a.** hammer
- ○ **b.** plumber
- ○ **c.** tighten
- ○ **d.** toolbox
- ○ **e.** hardware

3. tardy : late : : dialogue : _____
- ○ **a.** play
- ○ **b.** two
- ○ **c.** discuss
- ○ **d.** speech
- ○ **e.** conversation

4. herd : cow : : flock : _____
- ○ **a.** bird
- ○ **b.** group
- ○ **c.** farm
- ○ **d.** family
- ○ **e.** gather

5. cat : tame : : leopard : _____
- ○ **a.** wild
- ○ **b.** tiger
- ○ **c.** jungle
- ○ **d.** spotted
- ○ **e.** dangerous

6. dog : bark : : bird : _____
- ○ **a.** nest
- ○ **b.** wing
- ○ **c.** flutter
- ○ **d.** chirp
- ○ **e.** fly

7. grubby : dirt : : greasy : _____
- ○ **a.** slippery
- ○ **b.** soap
- ○ **c.** dry
- ○ **d.** engine
- ○ **e.** oil

8. education : professor : : sports : _____
- ○ **a.** student
- ○ **b.** coach
- ○ **c.** teacher
- ○ **d.** knowledge
- ○ **e.** tennis

9. fruit : apple : : vehicle : _____
- ○ **a.** drive
- ○ **b.** car
- ○ **c.** travel
- ○ **d.** wheel
- ○ **e.** transportation

10. jockey : horse : : pilot : _____
- ○ **a.** fly
- ○ **b.** sky
- ○ **c.** airplane
- ○ **d.** captain
- ○ **e.** passenger

11. quilt : bed : : curtain : _____
- ○ **a.** blind
- ○ **b.** shade
- ○ **c.** fabric
- ○ **d.** window
- ○ **e.** hang

12. thermometer : temperature : : scale : _____
- ○ **a.** size
- ○ **b.** amount
- ○ **c.** degrees
- ○ **d.** pound
- ○ **e.** weight

2   Punctuation

Some questions test your knowledge of punctuation rules. Look at the sample.

SAMPLE: Read the group of words and look at the punctuation marks that follow. Decide which punctuation mark has been left out of the group of words. If no punctuation mark is needed, choose answer **e.** Mark your answer.

"Pablo," said the director "you must learn your lines for this scene."

○ **a.** .   ○ **b.** ;   ○ **c.** "   ○ **d.** ,   ○ **e.** *none*

Strategy

1. Read the group of words. Do you notice that any punctuation is missing?

2. Look at each answer. Think about the possible ways in which the punctuation mark can be used. Do any of these uses apply to the group of words?

3. Remember that end punctuation marks (periods, question marks, and exclamation points) are used to end sentences. (Periods, of course, are also used in abbreviations.) Therefore, an end punctuation mark will be the correct answer only if there is no punctuation at the end of a sentence, if a group of words is a run-on sentence, or if an abbreviation is missing a period.

4. Remember that quotation marks are always used in pairs—at the beginning and at the end of a quotation; therefore, a quotation mark will be the correct answer only if the group of words contains an odd number of quotation marks.

5. Remember that some groups of words will not need additional punctuation. Before you choose answer **e,** however, double-check that none of the punctuation marks could be used in the group of words.

Now look at the sample again. In a direct quotation, a comma should be used to separate the quoted words from the other words in the sentence. In this sentence, the comma is missing after the word *director.* The correct answer is **d.**

Practice: Punctuation

Read the group of words and look at the punctuation marks that follow. Decide which punctuation mark has been left out of the group of words. If no punctuation mark is needed, choose answer **e**. Mark your answer.

1. The tour bus stopped in Milan, Ohio the home of Thomas Edison, the inventor.
   ○ **a.** ( )   ○ **b.** ;   ○ **c.** :   ○ **d.** ,   ○ **e.** *none*

2. Clay thinks it's childish to wave at the caboose of a train but he does it anyway.
   ○ **a.** ,   ○ **b.** :   ○ **c.** "   ○ **d.** ;   ○ **e.** *none*

3. "Ms. O'Brien, where were you on the evening of June 22, 1987, at approximately seven oclock?"
   ○ **a.** .   ○ **b.** ,   ○ **c.** '   ○ **d.** :   ○ **e.** *none*

4. During the press conference, a reporter asked, "Mr Mayor, are you planning to run again?"
   ○ **a.** ( )   ○ **b.** "   ○ **c.** –   ○ **d.** .   ○ **e.** *none*

5. The math teacher handed out the diplomas, and the principal shook each students hand.
   ○ **a.** ,   ○ **b.** :   ○ **c.** '   ○ **d.** ;   ○ **e.** *none*

6. After seeing the musical *West Side Story,* Jill kept singing the songs "Somewhere" and "Tonight."
   ○ **a.** "   ○ **b.** ,   ○ **c.** '   ○ **d.** ?   ○ **e.** *none*

7. The ingredients for the chili included onions, beans and tomatoes.
   ○ **a.** :   ○ **b.** ;   ○ **c.** ,   ○ **d.** ?   ○ **e.** *none*

8. A battered sports car was parked by the curb I knew that Curt must be inside the house.
   ○ **a.** "   ○ **b.** ?   ○ **c.** ,   ○ **d.** ;   ○ **e.** *none*

9. The sunset contained the following colors green, pink, and yellow.
   ○ **a.** :   ○ **b.** ;   ○ **c.** ,   ○ **d.** .   ○ **e.** *none*

10. "Look up Fred's new telephone number, said Mr. Yee. "It's in my blue address book."
    ○ **a.** ,   ○ **b.** "   ○ **c.** ( )   ○ **d.** '   ○ **e.** *none*

11. What a welcome sight daffodils are They announce the beginning of spring.
    ○ **a.** .   ○ **b.** ?   ○ **c.** !   ○ **d.** ,   ○ **e.** *none*

12. An abacus, which is a type of simple counting device, contains beads strung on wires.
    ○ **a.** '   ○ **b.** ( )   ○ **c.** —   ○ **d.** ?   ○ **e.** *none*

3 Usage

Some items test your knowledge of how to use language correctly. Look at the sample.

SAMPLE: Read the sentences below. Choose the line that has an error in usage. If there are no mistakes, choose answer **d.** Mark your answer.

○ **a.** Matthew came in from working

○ **b.** in the garden. He lay

○ **c.** his work gloves on a bench.

○ **d.** *(No mistakes)*

Strategy

1. Read the item through once to become familiar with it.

2. Read it slowly a second time, looking for errors. Common usage errors include the following: confusing words such as *affect* and *effect,* incorrect verb forms and tenses, errors in subject-verb agreement, dangling modifiers, double negatives, incorrect forms of adjectives and adverbs, incorrect forms of pronouns, fragments, and run-ons.

3. Once you have found what you think is an error, double-check your answer by figuring out how you could correct it.

4. Remember that some items may not contain any errors. Before you mark answer **d,** however, reread the item. Make sure that you have checked for all of the types of usage errors listed above.

Now look at the sample again. The words *lie* and *lay* and their past forms are frequently confused. In this sentence, the word *lay* (meaning "to put down") rather than *lie* (meaning "to rest or recline") should be used. The past tense form should be used to agree with the past tense verb form in the first sentence *(came)*. The past tense of *lay* is *laid.* The answer is **b** since the verb is incorrect in this line.

Test-taking Strategies

Practice: Usage

Read the sentences below. Choose the line that has an error in usage. If there are no mistakes, choose answer **d.** Mark your answer.

1. ○ **a.** Elena and I put
   ○ **b.** sandwiches in baskets made of Swiss cheese
   ○ **c.** for the picnic.
   ○ **d.** *(No mistakes)*

2. ○ **a.** People shouldn't ought to
   ○ **b.** express opinions that hurt the
   ○ **c.** feelings of others.
   ○ **d.** *(No mistakes)*

3. ○ **a.** Neither rubber nor glass
   ○ **b.** is a good conductor of
   ○ **c.** electrical current.
   ○ **d.** *(No mistakes)*

4. ○ **a.** The detective announced,
   ○ **b.** "Nobody hasn't entered or left
   ○ **c.** the house since dawn."
   ○ **d.** *(No mistakes)*

5. ○ **a.** Atmospheric conditions effect
   ○ **b.** how well a radio signal is
   ○ **c.** received at a given point.
   ○ **d.** *(No mistakes)*

6. ○ **a.** When I went camping,
   ○ **b.** I took less pots
   ○ **c.** than Sue did.
   ○ **d.** *(No mistakes)*

7. ○ **a.** Those types of dogs were bred
   ○ **b.** to perform tasks such as herding
   ○ **c.** sheep and hunting rats.
   ○ **d.** *(No mistakes)*

8. ○ **a.** Because of the rain.
   ○ **b.** The class picnic will
   ○ **c.** not be held.
   ○ **d.** *(No mistakes)*

9. ○ **a.** After running for five miles and
   ○ **b.** bicycling for ten, the athletes
   ○ **c.** swum the length of the lake.
   ○ **d.** *(No mistakes)*

10. ○ **a.** Jeremy thought he did terrible
    ○ **b.** at the audition, but he was
    ○ **c.** cast as the lead in the play.
    ○ **d.** *(No mistakes)*

11. ○ **a.** Mel and I are identical twins,
    ○ **b.** but him and I are opposites in
    ○ **c.** everything but appearance.
    ○ **d.** *(No mistakes)*

12. ○ **a.** Beware of this town on
    ○ **b.** Saturdays, when crowds of
    ○ **c.** tourists comes in from the city.
    ○ **d.** *(No mistakes)*

13. ○ **a.** The students chosen to greet
    ○ **b.** the President and Vice-President
    ○ **c.** were Annette Ricci and me.
    ○ **d.** *(No mistakes)*

14. ○ **a.** The most awfullest thing
    ○ **b.** happened to Bob. His dog
    ○ **c.** actually ate his homework!
    ○ **d.** *(No mistakes)*

15. ○ **a.** Grass is less easily mown
    ○ **b.** when it is damp than when
    ○ **c.** it is perfectly dry.
    ○ **d.** *(No mistakes)*

16. ○ **a.** The Bombacis would of
    ○ **b.** gone to the rodeo if their
    ○ **c.** car hadn't had engine trouble.
    ○ **d.** *(No mistakes)*

4 Reading Comprehension: Main Idea

One common type of test question asks you to identify the main idea of a passage. The main idea may be stated or it may be implied. Look at the sample.

SAMPLE: Read the passage. Then choose the correct answer to the question. Mark your answer.

A hospital emergency room provides fast and expert treatment. People suffering from serious medical emergencies such as heart attacks, as well as people with minor injuries or illnesses such as sore throats or fevers, can be treated there. Some people come to the emergency room because they have no family doctor. Others come because they fall ill at night or because the hospital is the nearest center for medical attention. Yet others come to a hospital emergency room when they are away from home and do not know a local doctor. Some people go to a hospital because they know they will find, all in one location, not only doctors' services but also equipment for diagnosing ailments.

What is the main idea of the paragraph?

○ **a.** An emergency room provides expert treatment.

○ **b.** Some people have no family doctor.

○ **c.** A hospital emergency room provides expert treatment for people who come for different reasons and have different kinds of ailments.

○ **d.** Emergency rooms offer more complete medical services than family doctors.

Strategy

1. First check to see if the main idea is stated directly. Look at the opening or closing sentences of the passage, but remember that a main idea statement can be located anywhere in the passage.

2. If none of the sentences in the passage sums up the passage as a whole, the main idea is implied. Look at the four answer choices. Some of them may be details from the passage. Others may be ideas that are not supported by the information in the passage or ones that do not cover all of the information in the passage. Look for the sentence that best describes the most important points in the passage.

Now look at the sample again. In this example, there is no stated main idea that sums up all of the information presented in the paragraph. The main idea is implied. The first answer, **a,** is an important idea, but it does not sum up the services of a hospital emergency room and the reasons why people go there rather than to their own doctors. Answer **b** is a detail. Answer **c** sums up the services of emergency rooms *and* the reasons why people go there. Answer **d** is an idea but is not supported by the information in the passage. The correct answer is **c**.

Practice: Reading Comprehension

Read each passage. Then choose the correct answer to the question. Mark your answer.

Have you ever heard of Maurice Micklewhite? Walter Matuschanskayasky? Reginald Dwight? These names might not be familiar, but the faces that go with them are. These three number among the scores of famous people who changed their names at the beginning of their careers. The reasons for such name changes are many: perhaps the original name was too difficult to pronounce, or it wasn't "glamorous" enough. Whatever the cause, the end result is usually a mixture of truth and make-believe. And just in case you're wondering—those three names belong, respectively, to actors Michael Caine and Walter Matthau and rock star Elton John.

1. What is the main idea of the paragraph?

   ○ **a.** Two famous actors and a rock star changed their original names.
   ○ **b.** Some people change their names because they are difficult to pronounce.
   ○ **c.** Changing your name is an important key to success and fame.
   ○ **d.** Many famous people changed their names when they started their careers.

The surface of the swamp was as smooth and dark as molasses. It looked as though nothing had disturbed the muddy water for hundreds of years. Just a few feet below, weird-looking fish swam in frantic circles. Millions of microscopic animals hung suspended in the water. An alligator moved silently through the dark depths while tall weeds waved in its wake.

2. What is the main idea of the paragraph?

   ○ **a.** The swamp looked pretty, but it was full of dangerous animals.
   ○ **b.** Weird-looking fish swam in circles underneath the swamp's surface.
   ○ **c.** The swamp was teeming with life and activity.
   ○ **d.** A swamp breeds some of the strangest creatures ever known.

In ancient Greece, the color yellow was used to symbolize air. The great Italian artist Leonardo da Vinci wrote that yellow signified earth. For the Hopi of North America, yellow equals north, while the Navaho people believe that yellow is the color of the western mountains and thus brings twilight. Some societies use yellow to mean caution, as in yellow traffic lights and the painted lines used to divide roads.

3. What is the main idea of the paragraph?

   ○ **a.** Yellow has always been a symbol for the earth.
   ○ **b.** The ancient Greeks used the color yellow to symbolize air.
   ○ **c.** Yellow always symbolizes a geographical feature.
   ○ **d.** The color yellow has symbolized many things throughout history.

Answer Key

Analogies

(page 54)

1. c
2. d
3. e
4. a
5. a
6. d
7. e
8. b
9. b
10. c
11. d
12. e

Punctuation

(page 56)

1. d
2. a
3. c
4. d
5. c
6. e
7. c
8. d
9. a
10. b
11. c
12. e

Usage

(page 58)

1. b
2. a
3. d
4. b
5. a
6. b
7. d
8. a
9. c
10. a
11. b
12. c
13. d
14. a
15. d
16. a

Reading Comprehension

(page 60)

1. d
2. c
3. d

Test-taking Strategies

Part III: Unit-by-Unit Resources

This Part contains Resource Masters for each unit in your Student Book.

LANGUAGE AND USAGE UNITS

Parent Letters

These letters are in both English and Spanish. They provide a brief and simple introduction to the unit's subject matter and suggest one or more activities that parents can do with your students to reinforce the skills of the unit.

Games

A Game reinforces one of the skills taught in the Student Book. You may use these games throughout the year for review and to maintain skill levels. You will find them especially useful for LEP students.

LITERATURE AND WRITING UNITS

Parent Letters

These letters are in both English and Spanish. They provide a brief and simple introduction to the unit's subject matter and suggest one or more activities that parents can do with your students to reinforce the skills of the unit.

Writing About the Literature

This feature presents additional writing ideas for each literature selection in the Student Book. The ideas cover a broad range of types of writing: reports, poems, comparisons, letters. They supplement the ideas in your Student Book.

Prewriting Ideas

These warm-up activities supplement the ideas and activities in your Student Book. Use these to help students (1) choose a topic to write about and (2) focus and explore their topic.

Games

A Game reinforces one of the skills taught in the Student Book. You may use these games throughout the year for review and to maintain skill levels. You will find them especially useful for LEP students.

Writing Prompts

You will find two Writing Prompts for each type of writing taught in the Writing Process lessons in the Student Book. These prompts are intended to be used for assessment—either your own or as preparation for school- or district-wide tests.

These Prompts should not be used instead of prewriting activities. Whenever possible within curriculum demands, students' writing should be on topics of their own choosing.

(continued)

Writing Prompts *(continued)*

Diagnostic use: Use either Prompt for a quick in-class writing assignment before you begin the Writing Process for that type of writing. The resulting papers should not be graded but used to identify the skills students need to master.

Test-taking practice: Use either Prompt for practice in test-taking after you have completed the Writing Process lessons for a particular type of writing. Tell students how much time they will have, and remind them to pace themselves as they explore their topics, write, revise, and proofread.

Assessment: Use a pair of Prompts—Prompt I at the beginning of the year and Prompt II at the end—to assess progress in writing proficiency in your class, your school, or your district. Evaluate the papers holistically. (See pages 24–27.)

As an alternative, give the same assignment at the beginning and at the end of the year. In this case, you should mix the sets of papers so that evaluators do not know which paper was written first. You could compare scores for each student, for the class as a whole, or for the school or district.

Prewriting Masters

A set of two Prewriting Masters, I and II, is provided for each Writing Process prewriting lesson. Prewriting Master II matches a specific activity on the Ideas for Getting Started page in the Student Book.

Evaluation Masters

The **Self-evaluation Master** should be put into students' writing folders and used at three separate checkpoints: after revising, after proofreading, and after making a final copy. The master should be completed and used as a basis for corrections *before* the teacher evaluates the finished product.

Peer Evaluation Masters are to be used with writing conferences by students working in pairs or in groups.

The **Teacher Evaluation Master** assesses the same skills as those on the Self-evaluation Masters. See pages 20–21 for instructions on how to create analytic scales. HOUGHTON MIFFLIN ENGLISH recommends that a greater weight be given to content skills (under the Revising head) than to the skills listed under Proofreading and Final Copy.

The **Conversion Table** gives you a convenient formula to report scores as letter grades or percents.

Houghton Mifflin
English

Dear Parent,

Your child's English class is beginning a language and usage unit in HOUGHTON MIFFLIN ENGLISH entitled "The Sentence." In this unit, your child will learn how sentences are formed and how to write sentences that are correct, clear, direct, and varied.

"The Sentence" is one of eight grammar units. The other units focus on nouns, verbs, modifiers, capitalization and punctuation, pronouns, phrases, and clauses.

You can help to reinforce the skills your child is learning by practicing them at home. You might want to try the activities below or make up some of your own.

Family Activities

- Have your child tell you five sentences describing everyday activities of people in your family. (For example: *I get up at seven. Susan gets up at six.*) Then have your child change declarative sentences (sentences that make statements, such as the ones above) to interrogatives (ones that ask questions, such as *Do I get up at seven?*); to imperatives (ones that make commands, such as *Get up*); and to exclamations *(How I love to get up early!).*

- Using the sentences generated in the first activity, ask your child to try varying sentence length by combining some sentences *(I get up at seven, but Susan gets up at six).*

Please feel free to contact me about any questions you may have about the skills or activities covered in this unit.

Sincerely,

Unit 1 • Parent Letter

Houghton Mifflin
English

LEVEL 8

Estimado padre o madre,

La clase de inglés de su hijo o hija comienza una unidad de gramática en HOUGHTON MIFFLIN ENGLISH titulada *The Sentence (La oración).* En esta unidad, él o ella aprenderá cómo se forman las oraciones y cómo se escriben oraciones correctas, claras, directas y variadas.

The Sentence es una de ocho unidades sobre gramática y corrección. Las demás unidades se concentran en los sustantivos, los verbos, los modificadores, las mayúsculas y la puntuación, los pronombres, las frases, y las cláusulas.

Usted puede ayudar a reforzar las destrezas que aprende su hijo o hija, practicándolas en el hogar. Quizás le interese probar las siguientes actividades, o crear algunas de su propia invención.

Actividades para la familia

- Pídale a su hijo o hija que le formule cinco oraciones que describan las actividades cotidianas de las personas de la familia. (Por ejemplo: *I get up at seven.* —Me despierto a las siete. *Susan gets up at six.* —Susan se despierta a las seis.) Luego pídale que cambie las oraciones declarativas (oraciones que afirman algo, como las dos anteriores) en oraciones interrogativas (las que preguntan, como *Do I get up at seven?* —¿Me despierto a las siete?); en oraciones imperativas (las que ordenan, como *Get up.* —Despierta); y en oraciones exclamativas (*How I love to get up early!* —¡Cómo me gusta despertar temprano!).

- Usando las oraciones que generaron en la primera actividad, pídale a su hijo o hija que varíe la extensión de las oraciones, juntando algunas de ellas (*I get up at seven, but Susan gets up at six.* —Yo me despierto a las siete, pero Susan se despierta a las seis).

Sienta la libertad de comunicarse conmigo sobre cualquier pregunta que tenga sobre las destrezas o actividades que se presentan en esta unidad.

Sinceramente,

SENTENCE MedLeY

simple	compound	complex	simple	compound	complex
compound	complex	simple	compound	complex	simple
complex	simple	compound	complex	simple	compound

Objective
To create and identify simple, compound, and complex sentences

Players
Any number

You will need
A sentence grid (on the next page); pencil and paper for each player

Before you play
1. Choose a leader to copy the sentence grid onto the chalkboard or a large piece of poster board. The leader is also the timekeeper and scorekeeper.
2. Choose 2 judges to make decisions if players challenge each other's sentences.

How to play
1. The leader places the sentence grid where it can be seen easily by all the players.
2. Working independently, players have 10 minutes to use the words in the grid in as many sentences as possible. (*Only* those words can be used.) Players must then label each sentence *simple, compound,* or *complex*.
3. When the time is up, each player reads his or her sentences aloud. Other players can challenge any sentences that are not complete, that are labeled incorrectly, or that contain words not on the grid.

Scoring
A player earns 1 point for each simple sentence, 2 points for each compound sentence, and 3 points for each complex sentence. The player with the most points wins the round.

Variation
Players can make their own sentence grids by writing a simple subject, a simple predicate, a coordinating conjunction, or a subordinating conjunction in each block. The blank grid on the next page can be used for this game variation.

Unit 1 • Game

SENTENCE MedLeY

simple	compound	complex	simple	compound	complex
compound	complex	simple	compound	complex	simple
complex	simple	compound	complex	simple	compound

Sentence grid

you	as	blew	when	a
rain	watched	drifted	sidewalk	on
but	snow	and	fell	left
wind	slept	I	the	after
shoveled	if	we	howled	slipped

Blank grid (for variation of Sentence Medley)

Houghton Mifflin
English

LEVEL 8

Dear Parent,

Sharing our experiences with others is a large part of our daily lives. In this literature and writing unit in HOUGHTON MIFFLIN ENGLISH called "Personal Narrative," your child will discover how to write interesting stories about personal experiences.

After reading literature selections based on personal experiences and after practicing various skills, your child will write a personal narrative. Using the writing process and concentrating on one aspect of writing at a time, your child will complete these steps: choosing a topic (prewriting); writing a first draft; revising for content; proofreading for errors in spelling, grammar, capitalization, and punctuation; and making a final copy to share with classmates (publishing). Do not worry if your child comes home with drafts containing errors; these errors will be corrected in a later step.

To help your child become a better storyteller, you might want to try the activity below or make up one or two of your own.

Family Activity

- Help your child practice making up dialogue by asking him or her to supply a sentence that a family member or close friend might say in a given situation. Then have your child restate the sentence in the way that other family members would express the same idea. You might want to conduct an entire dinner conversation in which each family member converses as if he or she were another member of the family.

Please do not hesitate to contact me if you have any questions about the materials in this unit.

Sincerely,

Unit 2 • Parent Letter

Estimado padre o madre,

Compartir experiencias con los demás es una parte grande de nuestras vidas diarias. En esta unidad de literatura y redacción de HOUGHTON MIFFLIN ENGLISH, titulada *Personal Narrative (La narración personal)* su hijo o hija descubrirá cómo redactar cuentos interesantes sobre sus experiencias personales.

Después de leer las selecciones literarias basadas en experiencias personales y después de practicar varias destrezas, su hijo o hija escribirá una narración personal. Usando el proceso de redacción, en el que cada paso se concentra en un aspecto a la vez, su hijo o hija completará los siguientes pasos: escoger un tema; redactar un primer borrador; revisar el contenido del borrador; corregir los errores de ortografía, de gramática, de capitalización, y de puntuación; y crear una copia final (la publicación) para compartirla con los compañeros de clase. No se preocupe si su hijo o hija lleva al hogar borradores con errores; éstos se corregirán en una etapa más tarde.

Para ayudar a que su hijo o hija sea mejor cuentista, puede que a usted le interese probar las siguiente actividad o crear una o dos de su propia invención.

Actividad para la familia

■ Ayude a su hijo o hija a practicar inventar un diálogo, pidiéndole que invente una oración que podría decir un familiar o amigo íntimo en una determinada situación. Luego pídale que la cambie, expresándola en la forma en que la dirían otros familiares. Podrían llevar toda una conversación en la cena, en la que cada familiar habla como si él o ella fuera otro de los de la familia.

Por favor no demore en comunicarse conmigo si tiene alguna pregunta sobre los materiales de esta unidad.

Sinceramente,

Writing About the Literature

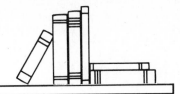

The Road Not Taken (page 54)

1. Pretend that you, unlike the narrator, took the well-traveled road. Twenty years later you decide to tell about your experiences. What were they? Write a story about some of your experiences along the well-traveled road of life.

2. What other symbols could be used for making choices? Write a poem about an important choice you have made, using your own symbol.

3. How did the writer's choice of taking the less-traveled road make a difference in his life? Write a first-hand report of an interview with the narrator twenty years after he made his choice.

Growing Up (page 56)

1. How would you define *gumption*? Russell's mother does not think that he has it. Pretend that you are Russell's father and you think Russell does have gumption. Write a dialogue between Russell's mother and father in which you, as Russell's father, defend your only son.

2. Do you have "gumption"? Write a personal narrative about an experience that showed this.

3. Pretend that you are Russell Baker. Write a poem about the road of life you did not take.

the drum (page 62)

1. The writer Henry Thoreau wrote these words in his book *Walden:*

    If a man does not keep pace with his companions, perhaps it is because he hears a different drummer. Let him step to the music which he hears, however measured or far away.

    How do you think these words might have inspired Nikki Giovanni in her poem "the drum"? Pretend that you are Giovanni and you have just read Thoreau's lines. Write a journal entry in which you express your feelings and opinions about Thoreau's words.

2. What particular experiences might have caused the narrator's father to offer the advice in the poem? Write a letter to your child in which you, the author's father, give these words of advice. Describe the experiences that led you to this conclusion.

3. Why do you suppose the author did not use capitalization or punctuation in this poem? Imagine that you are the author of "the drum." Write a letter to your editor justifying the style of your poem.

Prewriting Ideas: Personal Narrative

Use these prewriting ideas to help you find topics to write about. After you have chosen a topic, use the activities to help you focus, explore, or narrow your topic.

- **Brainstorming experiences**   Work alone or with a small group. List as fast as you can exciting, sad, happy, funny, or scary events in your life. What personal story ideas do you get?

- **Brainstorming places**   List as fast as you can notes about places you have visited that you like or dislike intensely. Then add why you went there and what happened to make you feel as you do.

- **Brainstorming people**   List as fast as you can notes about someone you like or dislike very much. Then give details about your experiences with that person.

- **Early-memory search**   Run an imaginary film of your life backward. Stop the reel at an important day and tell what you remember about it.

- **Free association**   Write the word you associate with *sports, music, money,* or *work.* Then write the next word that you associate with it. Create a chain of words that you can develop into a story about yourself.

- **Drawing**   Sketch a happy, sad, scary, or funny picture. Let it remind you of a personal experience. Then think about your experience as a story.

- **Being interviewed**   Pretend you are famous and are being interviewed on radio or television. Answer questions about outstanding events in your life.

- **Telling stories**   Tell a story about something you did. Keep the interest of your audience and encourage the listeners to ask questions.

- **Looking at art**   Look at paintings, photographs, or pictures in magazines and newspapers. Notice how each picture makes you feel. Then single out the most interesting picture and tell what experience in your life it reminds you of.

- **Diary and journal entries**   List interesting experiences you have written about in your diary. If you do not keep a diary, tell what you would include in one. The journal entries of famous people can give you ideas.

You Don't Say!

Objective
To reveal character traits through dialogue

Players
Any number, 2 on a team

You will need
Index cards; paper; pencils; a scorecard (on the next page)

Before you play
Brainstorm a list of famous pairs of characters, living or dead, real or imaginary (examples on the next page). Choose a leader who will write each pair on an index card and also keep score.

How to play
1. The leader shuffles the cards and hands 1 card to each team.
2. Each team has 10 (or 15) minutes to write a brief dialogue between the 2 characters, without using the characters' names. If possible, each character should have 2 speeches. For example, if the famous pair is Orville and Wilbur Wright, the players might write the following:

    "Well, brother, I'd like to ride in that contraption this time."

    "You may be a good bike rider, but this is quite another matter."

    "What could happen? The machine never gets too high off the ground, and there aren't many trees to hit here in Kitty Hawk."

    "I just don't want to damage something that took us so long to build."
3. Each team reads its dialogue to the group, with each player taking the part of a character.
4. After a team reads all of its dialogue, the other players try to guess the names of the characters.
5. Play continues until all teams have had a chance to read their dialogue.

Scoring
A team earns 5 points for guessing the identity of another team's characters. After the points have been tallied, a team *loses* 5 points if no one has guessed the names of their characters. The team with the most points wins.

Use with Composition Skills lesson, Writing Dialogue, p. 70

Famous pairs

Peter Pan and Wendy
Pinocchio and Gepetto
Romeo and Juliet
George and Martha Washington
Cinderella and the Prince
Dorothy and the Wizard of Oz
Tom Sawyer and Huckleberry Finn

Jack and Jill
Antony and Cleopatra
Hansel and Gretel
King Ferdinand and Queen Isabella
Ebenezer Scrooge and Bob Cratchit
Superman (Clark Kent) and Lois Lane
Abraham Lincoln and Mary Todd

Scorecard

NAMES OF TEAMS	POINTS						TOTAL

Writing a Personal Narrative • I

Directions: Write a personal narrative to share with your classmates about the most unusual or unexpected sight you ever saw. Was this sight a person or a thing? What did it look like? Did it have an unusual feel, smell, or taste? What did you say when you saw it? Did others have the same reaction? Where did you see it? in a museum? on the street? in a new place you were visiting?

Remember to

- have an attention-getting beginning
- include details that show rather than tell
- include dialogue
- have a good ending

Writing a Personal Narrative • II

Directions: Think about when you made something by yourself for the first time, when you accomplished something that made you feel proud and happy. Was it your first art project perhaps? your very first creation in the kitchen? Did it turn out just as you wanted it to, or did it have unexpected or amusing results? How did others view it or react to it? Write a personal narrative to share this achievement with your classmates.

Remember to

- have an attention-getting beginning
- include details that show rather than tell
- include dialogue to bring the scene to life
- have an ending that completes the action, shows rather than tells, fits the mood, and leaves readers feeling that they have been told just enough
- have sentences that are varied in length

Name _____ Date _____

Planning a Personal Narrative • I

Think of situations in your story that might have dialogue. List the people and the situations.

_____

_____

_____

_____

_____

Now create some dialogue to make your characters and story come alive!

The Writing Process, Step 1: Prewriting

Name _____ Date _____

Planning a Personal Narrative • II

Pretend that your story is a movie you have just seen. Tell a friend what happens in this movie. Try to make your friend see the movie just as you remember it. Choose one event. What details should you give?

The Writing Process, Step 1: Ideas for Getting Started, p. 75, "Talk About It"

Writing a Personal Narrative

Revising ☑

Did I make the beginning interesting? ☐
Did I include enough details? ☐
Did I use dialogue effectively? ☐
Did I make the ending interesting? ☐

Proofreading

Did I indent where necessary? ☐
Did I use capitals and punctuation correctly? ☐
Did I correct all fragments and run-ons? ☐
Did I spell all words correctly? ☐

Final Copy

Is my copy neat and accurate? ☐
Is my handwriting easy to read? ☐
Is my title capitalized correctly? ☐
Did I leave proper space for margins? ☐
Did I skip a line after my title? ☐

Unit 2 • Self-evaluation Master

The Writing Process, Steps 3, 4, 5

Your name _____

Writer's name _____

Writing a Personal Narrative

Questions ☑	Comments
1. Is the beginning interesting?	
2. Where could more details be added?	
3. Where could dialogue be added?	
4. Is the ending interesting?	

The Writing Process, Step 3: Revise

Student's name _____ Date _____

Personal Narrative: Analytic Scale

	poor	weak	good	very good	excellent
Revising Skills ☑					
Beginning is interesting	——	——	——	——	——
Details are included	——	——	——	——	——
Dialogue is effective	——	——	——	——	——
Ending is interesting	——	——	——	——	——
Proofreading Skills					
Paragraphs are indented	——	——	——	——	——
Capitals and punctuation used correctly	——	——	——	——	——
Fragments and run-ons corrected	——	——	——	——	——
Words spelled correctly	——	——	——	——	——
Final Copy Skills					
Neat and accurate	——	——	——	——	——
Easy to read	——	——	——	——	——
Title capitalized correctly	——	——	——	——	——
Margins properly spaced	——	——	——	——	——
Title followed by line of space	——	——	——	——	——

Comments:

Total score _____

Letter grade
or percent _____

Unit 2 • Teacher Evaluation Master

The Conversion Table on the next page will help you with scoring.
The Writing Process, Steps 3, 4, 5

Conversion Table

Scores	Letter Grade	Percent*
97–100	A+	_____
94–96	A	_____
90–93	A–	_____
83–89	B+	_____
77–82	B	_____
70–76	B–	_____
63-69	C+	_____
57–62	C	_____
50–56	C–	_____
43–49	D+	_____
37–42	D	_____
30–36	D–	_____
20–29	F	_____

*After you use the table to determine the letter grade, you can use your own school's system for reporting the percent that matches the letter grade.

Houghton Mifflin
English

Dear Parent,

Your child's English class is beginning a unit on nouns in HOUGHTON MIF-FLIN ENGLISH. In this unit, your child will practice using nouns in various forms. As your child learns more about nouns, including how to combine sentences with appositives and how to use exact nouns, your child's writing will improve.

To help reinforce the skills your child is learning, you might want to try the activities below or make up some of your own.

Family Activities

- Think of a category, such as *cars* or *clothing,* and have your child and other family members name exact nouns that fit the category. If you choose clothing, for example, someone may say *sweater.* Then ask that person to be even more specific by saying, for example, *cardigan* and *pullover.*

- While your child is reading a textbook or other material, ask him or her to name different kinds of nouns, for example, *common* (teacher), *proper* (Ms. Quinn), *compound* (homework), *collective* (group), *concrete* (book), and *abstract* (friendship).

If you have any questions about the skills or activities covered in this unit, do not hesitate to contact me.

Sincerely,

Unit 3 • Parent Letter

Estimado padre o madre,

La clase de inglés de su hijo o hija comienza una unidad sobre los sustantivos en HOUGHTON MIFFLIN ENGLISH. En esta unidad, él o ella practicará el uso de varios tipos de sustantivos en varias formas. Al aprender más sobre los sustantivos, incluyendo cómo juntar oraciones con apositivos y cómo usar los nombres específicos, mejorará lo que su hijo o hija escriba.

Para ayudar a reforzar las destrezas que aprende su hijo o hija, quizás le interese a usted probar las siguientes actividades o inventar algunas propias.

Actividades para la familia

- Piense en una categoría, como la de los automóviles o la de la ropa, y pídale a su hijo o hija y demás familiares que piensen en nombres precisos de la categoría que sea. Si escoge la ropa, por ejemplo, alguien podría decir *sweater* (suéter). Luego pídale a la persona que sea aún más precisa, diciendo, por ejemplo, *cardigan* (rebeca) o *pullover* (jersei).

- Mientras su hijo o hija lea un libro de texto u otro material, pídale que le nombre los diferentes tipos de sustantivos, por ejemplo, los *comunes* (*teacher* — maestro), los *propios* (Ms. Quinn), los *compuestos* (*homework* —tarea escolar), los *colectivos* (*group* —grupo), los *concretos* (*book* —libro), y los *abstractos* (*friendship* —la amistad).

Si tiene preguntas sobre las destrezas o actividades que se presentan en esta unidad, no demore en comunicarse conmigo.

Sinceramente,

Appositive

TRIVIA

Objective
To combine 2 sentences by changing one into an appositive

Players
2–4

You will need
Fifteen pairs of sentences (on the next page); tagboard strips; scissors; glue or tape

Before you play
1. Choose a leader to do the following: cut out and mount the sentences on tagboard, deal the cards to players, and keep score.
2. Choose 2 judges to rule on any combined sentence that is challenged.

How to play
1. The leader deals 3 cards to each player. The remaining cards go face down on the playing surface.
2. Players take turns drawing a card from the deck and discarding a card. They should look for matching pairs of sentences. One sentence in each pair should identify, describe, or rename a noun or pronoun that is in the other sentence.
3. When a matching pair is found, the player must combine the sentences orally by changing one sentence into an appositive. If other players challenge the sentence, the judges decide if the sentence is acceptable.
4. If the sentence pairs are successfully combined, the player sets aside those 2 cards and draws another card. If the combined sentence is judged unacceptable, the player keeps the cards and tries a different combination on another turn.
5. The game is over when there are no more cards to draw.

Scoring
A player earns 5 points for each pair that is successfully combined. The player with the most points is the winner.

Variation
Players can write their own sentence pairs and play Appositive Trivia with the new deck of cards.

Unit 3 • Game

Appositive TRIVIA

Sentence pairs

Leonardo da Vinci painted the Mona Lisa.	He was a famous artist and inventor.
Jupiter has seventeen moons.	It is the largest planet.
Rip Van Winkle slept for twenty years.	He is a character created by Washington Irving.
A persimmon has an orange-red color.	It is a kind of fruit.
Mary Cassatt is well known for her scenes of mothers and children.	She was an American painter.
Herman Melville wrote Moby Dick.	It is a novel about a white whale.
Mount Everest is 29,028 feet above sea level.	It is the world's highest peak.
John Chapman planted apple trees.	He was also known as Johnny Appleseed.
The cheetah can run 70 miles per hour.	It is the fastest land animal.
The stomach is below the esophagus.	It is part of the digestive system.
Honolulu is on the island of Oahu.	It is the capital of Hawaii.
Martina Navratilova won many Wimbledon championships.	She is a famous tennis player.
Isabella sponsored Columbus.	She was the queen of Spain.
The blue whale is an endangered species.	It is the largest mammal.
Margaret Mitchell wrote Gone With the Wind.	It is a novel about the Civil War.
A bulldozer can clear or level land.	It is a type of tractor.
The Pacific Ocean covers 70 million square miles.	It is the earth's largest body of water.

Unit 3 • Game

Houghton Mifflin
English

Dear Parent,

Almost any two items are alike in some ways and different in others, but it may take a keen eye to discover these similarities and differences. Your child is beginning a literature and writing unit in HOUGHTON MIFFLIN ENGLISH called "Comparison and Contrast." As your child prepares to write a paragraph of comparison and contrast, he or she will practice skills such as organizing a paragraph, writing a topic sentence, and supporting a main idea with details. Then, your child will write a paragraph of comparison and contrast, following the five steps of the writing process. Remember that your child's early drafts may contain errors in grammar and mechanics. These errors will be corrected during the proofreading step later on during the process of writing.

To reinforce the writing skills that your child will be learning, you may wish to complete the activity below or try one of your own.

Family Activity

- To help your child sharpen the ability to compare and contrast, ask him or her to name three similarities and three differences between two members of your family.

Encourage your child to share his or her work with you. If you have any questions about the skills or activities covered in this unit, please feel free to contact me.

Sincerely,

Unit 4 • Parent Letter

Houghton Mifflin
English

LEVEL 8

Estimado padre o madre,

Casi cualquier combinación de dos artículos presentará parecidos y diferencias, pero podría exigir una observación aguda descubrirlos. Su hijo o hija comienza una unidad de literatura y redacción de HOUGHTON MIFFLIN ENGLISH que se titula *Comparison and Contrast (La comparación y el contraste).* Después de las actividades de lectura, su hijo o hija practicará destrezas de escuchar, de hablar, y de pensar. Mientras su hijo o hija se prepara para escribir un párrafo de comparación y contraste, él o ella practicará destrezas que incluyen organizar un párrafo, escribir la oración principal de un párrafo, y apoyar la idea principal con detalles. Finalmente, su hijo o hija seguirá los cinco pasos del proceso de redacción. Recuerde que los primeros borradores de su hijo o hija podrán contener errores de gramática y de corrección. Estos se corregirán más tarde durante la etapa de corrección del proceso de redacción.

Para reforzar las destrezas de redacción que aprenderá su hijo o hija, quizás le interese a usted completar la siguiente actividad, o probar una de su propia invención.

Actividad para la familia

- Para ayudar a su hijo o hija a agudizar su habilidad de comparar y contrastar, pídale que nombre tres parecidos y tres diferencias entre dos familiares.

Anime a su hijo o hija para que comparta con usted su trabajo. Si usted tiene alguna preguntas sobre las destrezas o actividades que se presentan en esta unidad, por favor sienta la libertad de comunicarse conmigo.

Sinceramente,

Writing About the Literature

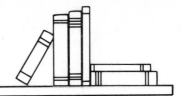

Icarus and Daedalus   (page 114)

1. "Icarus and Daedalus" illustrates the belief that people should avoid showing extreme ambition. What other extremes of behavior do you think people should avoid? Write a myth to explain your belief.

2. If Icarus could have told his story after his fall, what would he have said? Pretend that you are Icarus. Write a journal entry telling about how you felt after your fall.

3. What is a labyrinth? Have you ever felt that you were caught in one? Write a personal narrative about this experience.

4. Imagine that you are Daedalus and you are trying to warn your son Icarus about the dangers of being overly ambitious. Write a letter to your son giving him this advice. Support your opinion with examples from your own life.

An Introduction to Greek Mythology
(page 117)

1. Write a myth to explain the tides.

2. What is it like to be a Greek god? Pretend that you are Apollo. Describe your duties and tell which one you most enjoy.

3. You are an archaeologist, and you just dug up an ancient vase containing several articles used by ancient Greeks, as well as a scroll with writing that you can understand. What items did you find? What did the writing say? Write a press release to describe your findings.

4. Imagine that you are the Greek god who decided the fate of Icarus. Which god are you? Why did you decide that Icarus must drown? Write a letter to another god explaining why you caused the fall of Icarus.

Greek Gods and Mortals   (page 120)

1. Think of someone—a historical figure or a character in a book you have read— who showed *hubris*. Write a ballad—that is, a song that tells a story—about this person's achievements and ultimate fall or disaster.

2. Read any two Greek myths—one about the gods, and one about mortals. Choose a god and a mortal to compare and contrast. Write about how they are alike and different.

3. Read about some of the Greek gods. What were some of their specific characteristics? Imagine that you are a person living in ancient Greece. Write a paragraph or two about some godlike characteristics that you would like to have.

Prewriting Ideas:
Comparison and Contrast

Use these prewriting ideas to help you find topics to write about. After you have chosen a topic, use the activities to help you focus, explore, or narrow your topic.

- **Role-playing**   Pretend to be any person, place, idea, or object. Work with a partner, who will act as a second person, place, idea, or object. Perform a charade showing how you are alike and different.

- **Listing**   Quickly list pairs of things you would like to compare. Choose a pair that interests you. Then under the headings *Like* and *Different*, list the similarities and differences of the objects.

- **Reading**   Skim books, magazines, newspapers, advertisements, or other printed materials, and find people or things to compare. Then write notes about the similarities and differences of these people or things.

- **Drawing**   Draw a picture of two people or objects to show how alike and different they are. Then prepare a written list of these graphic details.

- **Observing**   Find people or things to compare by looking around your classroom, school, neighborhood, or home. Then note the ways they are alike and their differences.

- **Looking at art**   Find paintings, photographs, sculpture, architecture, drawings, or ceramics that differ in style. Then contrast and compare two or more pieces of art with different styles.

- **Show and tell**   Bring to class two objects, two photographs of different scenes, or a picture with many different people or objects. Then present to your class a comparison of two or more features of your display.

- **Watching television**   Think of contrasts in characters in a television program. Then write notes comparing these characters.

- **Interest inventory**   List people and activities that interest you. Then choose two and tell how they are alike and different.

...BuT What Do They HaVe in Common?

Objective
To compare objects

Players
4–10

You will need
Index cards; old magazines and newspapers; a scorecard (on the next page)

Before you play
Cut pictures of objects from magazines and newspapers, and mount each picture on an index card. Choose objects that represent a variety of categories, such as machines, furniture, plants, food, sporting equipment, animals, writing implements, tools, office supplies, articles of clothing, vehicles, containers, or musical instruments.

How to play
1. Choose one player to be the scorekeeper. He or she shuffles the cards, spreads them face up on the playing surface, and selects one object to start the play.
2. The first player chooses an object that has some similarity to the object the scorekeeper selected. The player then names as many similarities as possible. For example, if the scorekeeper starts the game with *eyeglasses*, the first player might choose an *automobile tire*. The player would then say that both are basically round, both are manufactured, both help a person perform a task.
3. The next player chooses an object that has some similarity to the object the first player selected and tells how those 2 objects are similar.
4. Players take turns selecting objects and explaining similarities.
5. After players name similarities for the objects they choose, other players may name additional similarities for those objects.
6. Play continues for a specified time or until all objects have been used.

Scoring
Players earn 1 point for each similarity named. The player with the most points is the winner.

Use with Composition Skills lesson, Organizing Comparison and Contrast Paragraphs, p. 130.

...BuT What Do They Have in Common ?

Scorecard

PLAYER	POINTS	POINTS	POINTS	TOTAL
1.				
2.				
3.				
4.				
5.				
6.				
7.				
8.				
9.				
10.				
11.				
12.				
13.				
14.				
15.				

Writing Comparison and Contrast • I

Directions: This picture shows how a penguin and a duck are alike in some ways and different in other ways. Write a paragraph to compare and contrast these animals for a friend. Give several ways in which the penguin and the duck are alike and several ways in which they are different.

Remember to

- include a topic sentence
- include a main idea with supporting details
- organize your comparison from details to conclusion or from conclusion to details
- include expressions like *similarly* and *however* to make your meaning clear
- include exact nouns

Writing Comparison and Contrast • II

Directions: The helicopter and the single-engine airplane in this picture are alike in some ways and different in others. Write a paragraph that compares and contrasts the helicopter and the single-engine airplane for a classmate.

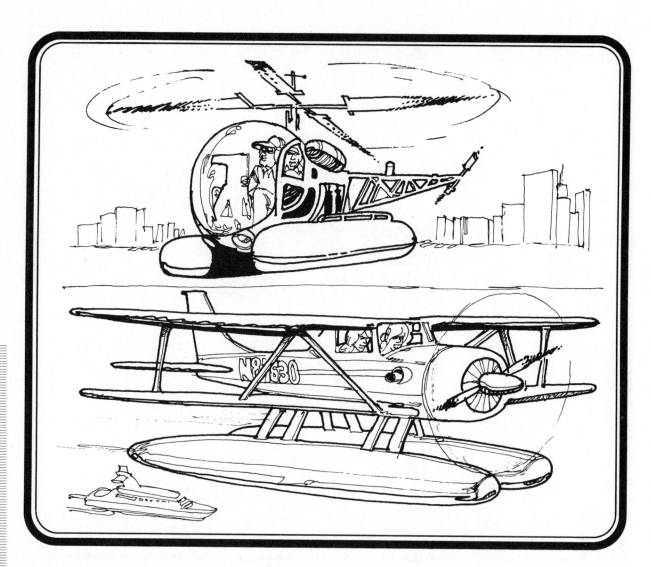

Remember to

- include a topic sentence
- include a main idea with supporting details
- organize your comparison from details to conclusion or from conclusion to details
- include expressions like *similarly* and *however* to make your meaning clear
- include exact nouns

Name _____ Date _____

Planning Comparison and Contrast • I

Think about the topics you are comparing and contrasting. What is the main idea of your first paragraph? Write it on the tabletop below. What are some details that support your main idea? Write them on the table legs.

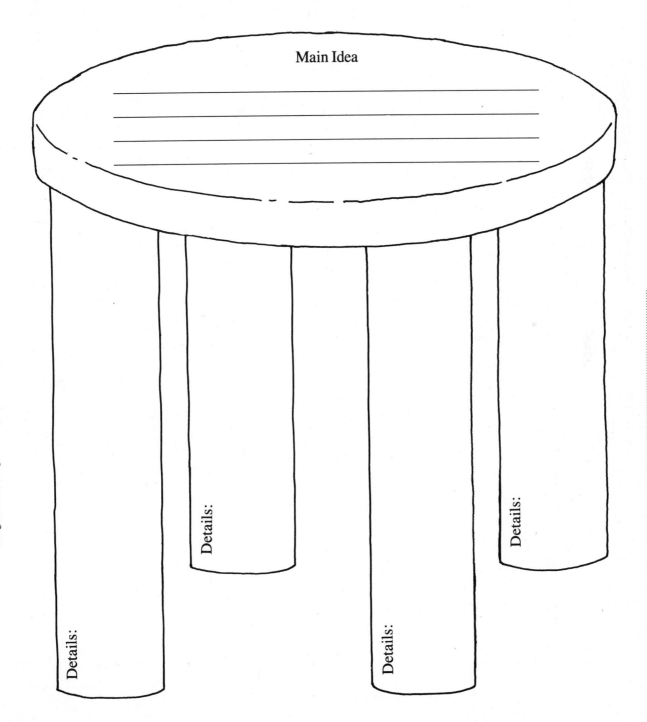

The Writing Process, Step 1: Prewriting

Name _____ Date _____

Planning Comparison and Contrast • II

Write the names of the two topics you are comparing. Below each topic, list
seven or eight characteristics. Draw red lines between the lists to connect similar
characteristics. Draw blue lines to connect interesting differences.

TOPIC: _____ TOPIC: _____

1. _____ 1. _____

_____ _____

2. _____ 2. _____

_____ _____

3. _____ 3. _____

_____ _____

4. _____ 4. _____

_____ _____

5. _____ 5. _____

_____ _____

6. _____ 6. _____

_____ _____

7. _____ 7. _____

_____ _____

8. _____ 8. _____

_____ _____

The Writing Process, Step 1: Ideas for Getting Started, p. 133, "Match Game"

Writing Comparison and Contrast

Revising ☑

Did I clearly state my main idea in a topic sentence? ☐

Do all my sentences support the main idea? ☐

Did I organize my details in a way that makes sense? ☐

Are my comparisons and contrasts clear? ☐

Proofreading

Did I indent where necessary? ☐

Did I capitalize correctly? ☐

Did I use possessive and plural nouns correctly? ☐

Did I use proper punctuation? ☐

Did I spell all words correctly? ☐

Final Copy

Is my copy neat and accurate? ☐

Is my handwriting easy to read? ☐

Is my title capitalized correctly? ☐

Did I leave proper space for margins? ☐

Did I skip a line after my title? ☐

Unit 4 • Self-evaluation Master

Your name _____

Writer's name _____

Writing Comparison and Contrast

Questions ☑	Comments
1. Is the main idea clearly stated in a topic sentence?	
2. Do all sentences support the main idea?	
3. Are details organized in a way that makes sense?	
4. Are comparisons and contrasts clear?	

The Writing Process, Step 3: Revise

Student's name _____ Date _____

Comparison and Constrast: Analytic Scale

	poor	weak	good	very good	excellent
Revising Skills ☑					
Main idea stated in topic sentence	——	——	——	——	——
Main idea supported with examples	——	——	——	——	——
Details sensibly organized	——	——	——	——	——
Comparisons and contrasts clear	——	——	——	——	——
Proofreading Skills					
Paragraphs are indented	——	——	——	——	——
Capitals used correctly	——	——	——	——	——
Possessive and plural nouns used correctly	——	——	——	——	——
Punctuation used correctly	——	——	——	——	——
Words spelled correctly	——	——	——	——	——
Final Copy Skills					
Neat and accurate	——	——	——	——	——
Easy to read	——	——	——	——	——
Title capitalized correctly	——	——	——	——	——
Margins properly spaced	——	——	——	——	——
Title followed by line of space	——	——	——	——	——

Comments:

Total score _____

Letter grade
or percent _____

Unit 4 • Teacher Evaluation Master

The Conversion Table on the next page will help you with scoring.
The Writing Process, Steps 3, 4, 5

Conversion Table

Scores	Letter Grade	Percent*
97–100	A +	_____
94–96	A	_____
90–93	A–	_____
83–89	B +	_____
77–82	B	_____
70–76	B–	_____
63-69	C +	_____
57–62	C	_____
50–56	C–	_____
43–49	D +	_____
37–42	D	_____
30–36	D–	_____
20–29	F	_____

*After you use the table to determine the letter grade, you can use your own school's system for reporting the percent that matches the letter grade.

Houghton Mifflin
English

LEVEL 8

Dear Parent,

Your child's English class is beginning a language and usage unit in HOUGHTON MIFFLIN ENGLISH called "Verbs." In this unit, your child will learn about different kinds of verbs, about forms and tenses of verbs, about voices of verbs, and about subject and verb agreement. Learning these skills will enable your child to write more clearly and effectively.

To help reinforce the skills your child is learning, try one or more of the activities below or make up some of your own.

Family Activities

- With your child, read an article from the sports or entertainment section of a newspaper. Have your child name all the verbs in the article and tell you their tenses.

- Find a newspaper article, write down the verbs on a separate sheet of paper, and then black out all the verbs in the article. Read the article with your child, having him or her provide verbs or even make up new ones to fill the spaces. Compare the new verbs with the original version for both choice of verb and verb tense or form.

If you have any questions about the skills or activities covered in this unit, please feel free to contact me.

Sincerely,

Unit 5 • Parent Letter

Houghton Mifflin
English

Estimado padre o madre,

La clase de inglés de su hijo o hija comienza una unidad de gramática en HOUGHTON MIFFLIN ENGLISH titulada *Verbs (Los verbos).* En esta unidad, su hijo o hija aprenderá sobre diferentes tipos de verbos, las formas y los tiempos verbales, las voces de los verbos, y sobre la concordancia entre sujeto y verbo. Aprender estas destrezas permitirá que su hijo o hija escriba más clara y eficazmente.

Para reforzar las destrezas que aprende su hijo o hija, prueben una o más de las siguientes actividades, o inventen alguna suya propia.

Actividades para la familia

- Junto con su hijo o hija, lea un artículo de la sección deportiva o de espectáculos de un periódico. Pídale a él o ella que señale todos los verbos del artículo, y que le diga qué tiempo y forma llevan.

- Busque un artículo de un periódico, escriba los verbos que contiene por separado en una hoja, y luego tache todos los verbos del artículo. Lea el artículo con su hijo o hija, pidiéndole que supla los verbos o incluso que invente verbos nuevos para llenar los espacios. Comparen los verbos nuevos con los de la versión original en cuanto a la selección del verbo en sí, y en cuanto al tiempo y la forma verbal.

Si tiene preguntas sobre las destrezas o actividades de esta unidad, por favor sienta la libertad de comunicarse conmigo.

Sinceramente,

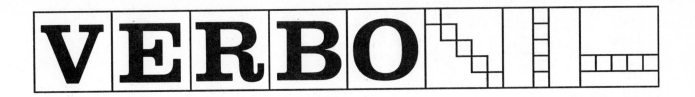

Objective
To identify action and linking verbs

Players
Any number

You will need
Unlined 4″ × 6″ index cards; tagboard or construction paper; pencils

Before you play
1. Each player prepares his or her own VERBO card by copying the bingo-like grid (on the next page) onto an index card. In each space, the player writes 1 of these terms: *action—transitive, action—intransitive,* or *linking*. (The terms should be used as equally as possible.)
2. Players cut up tagboard or construction paper to make game markers that will cover the spaces on the VERBO card.
3. Choose a leader to write sentences (samples on the next page) on 26 tagboard strips. Each sentence should be preceded by the letter *V, E, R, B,* or *O.*

How to play
1. The leader draws a sentence card, calls out the letter, and reads the sentence.
2. Players check their VERBO cards to see if they have a space labeled with the kind of verb that is in the sentence. If the player finds such a space, he or she writes the verb from the sentence on a game marker and places it over the space. For example, suppose the leader reads this sentence: *E—The batter struck out.* If a player has a space in the *E* column that is labeled *action— intransitive,* he or she writes *struck* on a marker and places it on the space.
3. The leader continues reading sentence cards until 1 of the players covers all the spaces in a row. Rows may be horizontal, vertical, or diagonal. When a player calls "VERBO!" the leader should check the card to be sure that all the verbs are correctly labeled.

Scoring
The first player to call "VERBO!" is the winner of the round (if his or her card has been correctly played). If several rounds are played, the winner of each round receives 10 points. The player with the most points wins the game.

Use with Lesson 1, Kinds of Verbs, p. 146.

VERBO

Sample sentences

1. I feel wonderful.
2. The apples taste sour.
3. A tree grows slowly.
4. Jill slammed the door.
5. No one answered the question.
6. Everyone arrived on time.
7. The runner finished last.
8. All remained calm.
9. A carpenter uses a saw.
10. Elephants are huge.
11. Rewrite the sentence.
12. Do not run in the corridor.
13. Dolphins can be useful.
14. The soup smelled delicious.
15. His shirt cost too much.
16. The sun sets earlier in the fall.
17. We rehearsed the play.
18. Tad forgot his lines.
19. The lake freezes in the winter.
20. You noticed the sign.
21. Tigers roam freely.
22. The audience clapped loudly.
23. He knows her name.
24. The dog appeared nervous.
25. Some whales have no teeth.
26. Workers dug a foundation.

V	E	R	B	O
		FREE SPACE		

Answers:

1. linking
2. linking
3. action—intrans.
4. action—trans.
5. action—trans.
6. action—intrans.
7. action—intrans.
8. linking
9. action—trans.
10. linking
11. action—trans.
12. action—trans.
13. linking
14. linking
15. action—trans.
16. action—intrans.
17. action—trans.
18. action—trans.
19. action—trans.
20. action—trans.
21. action—intrans.
22. action—intrans.
23. action—trans.
24. linking
25. linking
26. action—trans.

Houghton Mifflin
English

Dear Parent,

Most of us enjoy reading for pleasure. The two short stories that begin this literature and writing unit of HOUGHTON MIFFLIN ENGLISH called "Story" will provide pleasurable reading and will serve as writing models for your child. Using the five steps of the writing process, your child will incorporate skills learned in the unit to write a well-planned short story.

Encouraging your child to read more will foster his or her appreciation of literature and promote a facility for writing. With these goals in mind, you may wish to try one or more of the activities below with your child.

Family Activities

- Encourage your child to read by sharing what you read with him or her. Talk about your favorite character, an intriguing plot, or an exotic setting. Ask your child to share his or her reading experiences with you.

- Read a short story with your child. Ask your child to think of another beginning or ending to the story, a different setting or point of view, or a different twist to the plot. You both may have fun producing a new story!

Ask your child to share with you what he or she learns in this unit. Feel free to contact me if you have any comments or questions.

Sincerely,

Unit 6 • Parent Letter

Houghton Mifflin
English

Estimado padre o madre,

La mayoría disfrutamos de la lectura como diversión. Los dos cuentos con los que comienza esta unidad de literatura y redacción de HOUGHTON MIFFLIN ENGLISH que se titula *Story (El cuento),* le brindarán el placer de leer y servirán como modelos de redacción para su hijo o hija. Usando los cinco pasos del proceso de redacción, su hijo o hija incorporará las destrezas que ha aprendido en la unidad para escribir un cuento bien planificado.

Animar a su hijo o hija para que lea más desarrollará su aprecio por la literatura y promoverá una redacción más fácil. Con estos objetivos en mente, a usted quizás le interese probar una o más de las siguientes actividades.

Actividades para la familia

- Anime a su hijo o hija para que lea, compartiendo con él o ella lo que usted lee. Háblele de los personajes favoritos suyos, sobre una trama de intriga, o sobre algún ambiente exótico. Pídale que comparta con usted sus experiencias con la lectura.

- Lea un cuento junto con su hijo o hija. Pídale que piense en otro comienzo o desenlace para el cuento, en otro ambiente, en otro punto de vista, o en algún suceso sorpresivo dentro de la trama. ¡Es posible que disfruten ambos de producir un cuento nuevo!

Pídale a su hijo o hija que comparta con usted lo que él o ella aprende en esta unidad. Sienta la libertad de comunicarse conmigo si usted tiene alguna observación o pregunta.

Sinceramente,

Unit 6 • Parent Letter

Writing About the Literature

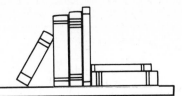

The Two Brothers   (page 204)

1. Think of a proverb or a maxim that you like. Write a parable to explain it.

2. Are you adventurous, like the younger brother, or cautious, like the older brother? Write a personal narrative that shows which brother you are like.

3. How is "The Two Brothers" like or different from "The Dinner Party"? Write two or three paragraphs comparing and contrasting the two stories. Show how the behavior of any one character from each story illustrates your opinion.

4. Imagine that you are a parent of the two brothers. Write a letter to one of the boys. Tell him about events in his childhood that showed the same kind of behavior he has just shown in "The Two Brothers."

5. Read about Leo Tolstoy to find out more about his attitude toward life. Then write a review of "The Two Brothers." Tell how the story succeeds or fails in expressing Tolstoy's ideas.

The Dinner Party   (page 207)

1. Imagine that you are the hostess. What were your thoughts and feelings when you first saw the cobra? Were you frightened? Were you tempted to warn the other guests? Write your journal entry for the evening of the dinner party.

2. What would have happened if the American naturalist had behaved differently? Rewrite the story. Be sure that your story has a conflict, a climax, and a resolution.

3. How do you suppose the colonel might have reacted to the hostess's act of self-control? Would he have changed his opinion about women? Write a dialogue that might have taken place between the young girl and the colonel after the end of the story.

4. Rewrite the story from the first-person point of view, using the American naturalist as narrator.

5. India was a British colony from the late 1700s until 1947. Find out more about that country. Choose one area to research—such as the geography, government, or history before or after the independence—and write a short research report.

Prewriting Ideas: Story

Use these prewriting ideas to help you find topics to write about. After you have chosen a topic, use the activities to help you focus, explore, or narrow your topic.

- **Reading**   Read stories in books and magazines. Note story ideas that occur to you. Choose and develop one idea.

- **Brainstorming settings**   Work alone, with a partner, or with a small group. Write as quickly as you can notes on interesting or faraway places where stories could take place.

- **Brainstorming characters**   List quickly characteristics you have observed in people. Then create characters for your story by clustering any of these characteristics. Add details of how they look, think, and act.

- **Brainstorming plots**   List ideas for problems for and outcomes of stories. Choose one problem for your characters. Then explain the solution to the problem.

- **Talking and listening in pairs**   Take turns telling your story ideas. Tell who the story is about and what will happen.

- **Free association**   Write the word that *challenge, excitement, difficulty,* or *reward* makes you think of. Then write the next word that comes to mind. Keep writing until a story idea begins to form.

- **Drawing**   Draw a scene that shows one or more people doing something. Then write what happens next.

- **Role-playing**   Pretend you are the main character in a story. Assign supporting roles to two or three classmates. Then act out the story.

- **Looking at art**   Look at paintings, drawings, and photographs. Then tell the stories you see in them.

- **Listening to music**   Play a favorite piece of music on an instrument or on the radio. Close your eyes and try to conjure up a scene the melody suggests. Then tell the story you have imagined.

- **Watching movies**   Think about the movies you have seen in the theater or on television. Then write ideas for your own story.

- **Photojournalism**   Scan a newspaper to find interesting stories and pictures. Read the stories and captions. Then think of a newsworthy feature story of your own.

Tale Spinning

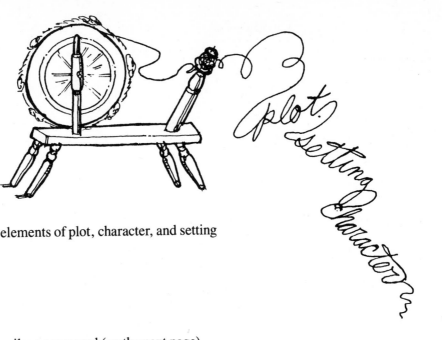

Objective
To create a story and identify elements of plot, character, and setting

Players
6–8

You will need
Two colors of index cards; pencils; a scorecard (on the next page)

Before you play
1. Using index cards of one color, each player writes on a card the name of a concrete object, such as *tree, wand,* or *sky.* All the cards go in a pile.
2. Choose a leader to label 9 cards of another color with the word *plot, character,* or *setting.* (Each label is written 3 times.)
3. The leader also can serve as scorekeeper and as a judge whenever necessary.

How to play
1. Player 1 draws 1 card from the object pile and 1 card from the story-element pile, showing the cards to the other players. He or she must use the name of the object in the first sentence of a story; the sentence also must contain the story element written on the other card. For example, a player who draws the words *tree* and *character* might say, "One sunny morning a young girl sat weeping under the branches of a towering elm tree."
2. Player 2 draws 2 cards—1 from each pile—and makes up a sentence that continues the story.
3. Other players may challenge a sentence if it seems unrelated to the story line or if the required story element is not developed.
4. If a player cannot think of a sentence, another player may take the cards and make his or her own response.
5. Play continues until all players have had a chance to add a sentence to the story. The last player tries to make up a resolution of the story conflict.

Scoring
Players earn 1 point for creating a sentence using the object and 1 point for developing the required element of plot, setting, or character. The last player earns an additional point for resolving the conflict. The player with the most points is the winner.

Tale Spinning

Scorecard

Players' Names	Points for Object	Points for Story Element	Points for Resolution	Total Points

Unit 6 • Game

Writing a Story • I

Directions: What are these two hikers doing? Why are they here? Are they searching for something or someone? Who or what might they be searching for? What will happen? Write a story about the picture.

Remember to

- choose an appropriate point of view
- include details that show your readers what your characters are like
- describe the setting, using details to help create the mood
- have a plot that includes a conflict, a climax, and a resolution

Writing a Story • II

Directions: Imagine that the tables were turned—that children went to work and parents went to school. Do you think that this situation would create any conflicts between children and their parents? What conflicts can you imagine? How would the children feel toward the parents? the parents toward the children? Write a story about the family in the picture. Share your story with your family and friends.

Remember to

- choose an appropriate point of view
- include details that show your readers what your characters are like
- describe the setting, using details to help create the mood
- have a plot that includes a conflict, a climax, and a resolution

Planning a Story • I

Think about the story you are writing. Use this diagram to work out the plot of your story. Write the conflict. Then write the rising action, the climax, and the resolution.

CLIMAX

RESOLUTION

RISING ACTION

3.

2.

1.

CONFLICT

Planning a Story • II

Make a detailed plan for your story idea. Write some of the details that you can think of for the setting and the main character. Then think about your plot. Write the events in order.

Setting

Time: _____

_____

Place: _____

Character

Looks _____

_____

_____

Acts _____

_____

_____

Says _____

_____

_____

_____

Plot

1. _____

_____

_____

2. _____

_____

_____

3. _____

_____

_____

4. _____

_____

_____

_____

The Writing Process, Step 1: Ideas for Getting Started, p. 223, "Plan Your Story"

Writing a Story

Revising ☑

Does my plot have a conflict? a climax? a resolution? ☐

Did I use dialogue, details, or actions to make the characters real? ☐

Did I use details effectively to show the setting? ☐

Did I use the same point of view throughout? ☐

Proofreading

Did I indent where necessary? ☐

Did I capitalize and punctuate correctly? ☐

Did I use the right verbs and verb forms? ☐

Did I spell all words correctly? ☐

Final Copy

Is my copy neat and accurate? ☐

Is my handwriting easy to read? ☐

Did I capitalize my title correctly? ☐

Did I leave proper space for margins? ☐

Did I skip a line after my title? ☐

Unit 6 • Self-evaluation Master

The Writing Process, Steps 3, 4, 5

Your name _____

Writer's name _____

Writing a Story

Questions ☑	Comments
1. Does the plot have a conflict? a climax? a resolution?	
2. Where could dialogue, details, and actions be used to make the characters more real?	
3. Do the details effectively show the setting?	
4. Is the same point of view used throughout?	

Student's name _____   Date _____

Story: Analytic Scale

	poor	weak	good	very good	excellent
Revising Skills ☑					
Conflict, climax, and resolution included in plot	____	____	____	____	____
Dialogue, details, actions make characters real	____	____	____	____	____
Details show setting effectively	____	____	____	____	____
Same point of view throughout	____	____	____	____	____
Proofreading Skills					
Paragraphs are indented	____	____	____	____	____
Capitals and punctuation used correctly	____	____	____	____	____
Verbs and verb forms used correctly	____	____	____	____	____
Words spelled correctly	____	____	____	____	____
Final Copy Skills					
Neat and accurate	____	____	____	____	____
Easy to read	____	____	____	____	____
Title capitalized correctly	____	____	____	____	____
Margins properly spaced	____	____	____	____	____
Title followed by line of space	____	____	____	____	____

Comments:

Total score _____

Letter grade
or percent _____

Unit 6 • Teacher Evaluation Master

The Conversion Table on the next page will help you with scoring.
The Writing Process, Steps 3, 4, 5

Conversion Table

Scores	Letter Grade	Percent*
97–100	A +	_____
94–96	A	_____
90–93	A–	_____
83–89	B +	_____
77–82	B	_____
70–76	B–	_____
63-69	C +	_____
57–62	C	_____
50–56	C–	_____
43–49	D +	_____
37–42	D	_____
30–36	D–	_____
20–29	F	_____

*After you use the table to determine the letter grade, you can use your own school's system for reporting the percent that matches the letter grade.

Houghton Mifflin
English

Dear Parent,

Your child's English class is about to begin a language and usage unit in HOUGHTON MIFFLIN ENGLISH called "Modifiers." In this unit, your child will practice using correct and exact modifiers that will add color, details, and clarity to his or her writing. Learning how to change the position of modifiers in a sentence will also add variety to your child's compositions.

To reinforce the skills in this unit, try one or more of the following activities with your child.

Family Activities

- Read some magazine ads with your child. Together, change the ads by substituting new modifiers that describe the same item. Which ads do you think are more effective?

- With your child, compose an ad describing an unnamed product. Ask other family members to guess what the product is. Are they right?

Do not hesitate to contact me if you have any questions about the materials in this unit.

Sincerely,

Unit 7 • Parent Letter

Houghton Mifflin
English

LEVEL 8

Estimado padre o madre,

La clase de inglés de su hijo o hija va a comenzar una unidad de gramática en HOUGHTON MIFFLIN ENGLISH que se titula *Modifiers (Los modificadores).* En esta unidad, su hijo o hija practicará el uso de palabras modificadoras correctas y precisas que añadirán color, detalles, y claridad a lo que escriba. Aprender a cambiar el lugar de los modificadores en una oración también añadirá variedad a las composiciones de su hijo o hija.

Para reforzar las destrezas de esta unidad, pruebe con su hijo o hija una o más de las siguientes actividades.

Actividades para la familia

- Lea algunos anuncios de una revista con su hijo o hija. Juntos, cambien los anuncios sustituyendo modificadores que describan el mismo artículo. ¿Cuál de los dos anuncios tiene más impacto?

- Con su hijo o hija, componga un anuncio que describa un producto que no se nombra. Pídanle a los demás de la familia que adivinen qué producto es. ¿Lo adivinaron?

No demore en comunicarse conmigo si usted tiene preguntas sobre las destrezas o actividades que se presentan en esta unidad.

Sinceramente,

Unit 7 • Parent Letter

120

Who Gets the SQUARE?

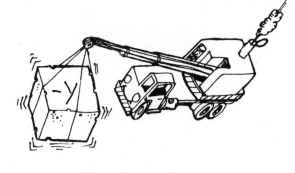

Objective
To create adjectives by adding suffixes to words

Players
2–4

You will need
Construction paper in as many colors as there are players; game board and 2 spinners (on the next page); 2 rivets or paper fasteners; pencils or pens

Before you play
1. If possible, make a larger game board by copying the model onto a large piece of tagboard or poster board.
2. Make 2 spinners from tagboard by using the patterns on the next page. Attach an arrow to each spinner with a rivet or paper fastener.
3. Each player chooses a different color construction paper and cuts out 14 game markers of about the same size as the squares on the game board. The following suffixes are then written on the markers: *-al, -an, -ar, -ary, -en, -ful, -ian, -ic, -ish, -like, -ly, -ous, -some,* and *-y.* (Players keep all 14 game markers face up at their place.)

How to play
1. Each player spins both spinners and moves to the indicated column and row. For example, if the first arrow lands on *B* and the other arrow lands on *3,* the player moves to the B column and then finds row 3 in that column. The player creates another word by adding 1 of the 14 suffixes to the word on the game board. He or she covers the word with the corresponding suffix game marker, says the word aloud, and spells it.
2. Other players can challenge any word that may not be formed correctly. If necessary, a dictionary can be checked.
3. Players alternate turns until 1 player uses all of his or her squares. That player is the winner.

Variation
Players can add more than 1 suffix to a word. For example, if the player lands on a square with the word *hand,* he or she could form the words *handy* and *handful* and cover the word with those two suffix markers.

Who Gets the SQUARE?

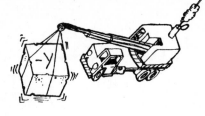

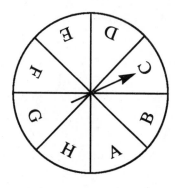

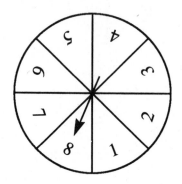

Game board

	A	B	C	D	E	F	G	H
1	fame	help	care	wind	pole	lone	hero	child
2	color	hope	wood	Italy	time	word	lump	fur
3	love	Russia	worth	pity	history	delight	beauty	origin
4	adventure	parent	globe	harm	Brazil	life	hair	study
5	fiction	worry	joy	marvel	bother	emotion	symbol	brown
6	comic	awe	poet	fear	alphabet	sun	self	myth
7	terrify	suburb	Canada	tire	talk	rain	home	continent
8	fun	reed	day	mystery	Alaska	steel	Paris	scholar

Houghton Mifflin
English

LEVEL 8

Dear Parent,

If a writer fails to use vivid description, it is difficult for us to picture what is being talked about. In this literature and writing unit in HOUGHTON MIFFLIN ENGLISH, your child will read a novel excerpt that is full of vivid details. He or she will then learn how to write a colorful description, choosing details that create a desired impression and using language that appeals to the reader's senses. To write this description, your child will proceed through the five steps of the writing process.

Don't be alarmed if you see early drafts of your child's paper filled with arrows, errors, and crossed-out words. Your child is probably already in the process of improving his or her paper. At various stages, your child will be working to improve both the content and the form of his or her paper. Your child needs your encouragement—from the unformed first draft to the corrected final copy.

To help sharpen your child's senses, you can reinforce the skills of this unit by doing the activity below at home.

Family Activity

- Ask your child to describe something that he or she would very much like to have. What color and shape would it have? What would it smell like? How would it taste? How would it feel to the touch?

If you have any questions about this unit, please feel free to contact me.

Sincerely,

Unit 8 • Parent Letter

Estimado padre o madre,

Si un escritor no usa descripciones con vida, es difícil que nos podamos imaginar de lo que habla. En esta unidad de literatura y redacción de HOUGHTON MIFFLIN ENGLISH, su hijo o hija leerá una selección de una novela que está llena de detalles con vida. Luego, él o ella aprenderá a redactar una descripción llena de colorido, a escoger detalles que crean la impresión que uno busca, y a usar palabras que apelan a los sentidos del lector. Para escribir esta descripción, su hijo o hija pasará por los cinco pasos del proceso de redacción.

No se preocupe si los primeros borradores del trabajo de su hijo o hija aparecen con partes tachadas, con flechas, y con errores. El o ella probablemente ya está en el proceso de mejorar su trabajo escrito. En varias etapas, su hijo o hija trabajará para mejorar tanto el contenido como la forma de su trabajo escrito. El o ella necesita el aliento suyo, desde el primer borrador rústico hasta la copia final corregida.

Para ayudar a agudizar los sentidos de su hijo o hija, usted puede reforzar las destrezas de esta unidad llevando a cabo una de las siguientes actividades en el hogar.

Actividad para la familia

- Pídale a su hijo o hija que le describa algo que a él o a ella le gustaría mucho tener. ¿De qué color es, y qué forma tiene? ¿Qué olor podría tener? ¿Qué sabor podría tener? ¿Cómo se sentiría al tacto?

Si tiene alguna pregunta sobre esta unidad, por favor sienta la libertad de comunicarse conmigo.

Sinceramente,

Unit 8 • Parent Letter

Writing About the Literature

First Time Aloft   (page 270)

1. Imagine that you are Buttons and that you have just climbed the main-skysail. How do you feel? Are you happy? proud? eager to repeat the experience? Write a poem describing your feelings during your climb. Try to use figurative language.

2. What was the most startling and impressive natural sight you ever saw? Was it a lonely beach on a cold winter day? a sunrise or a sunset? a forbidding and angry ocean during a storm? What did you see? hear? smell? touch? taste? Write a description of the picture left by this experience in your mind's eye.

3. What does Buttons look like in your mind's eye? Do you picture him as he appears in the drawing in your textbook? What is his facial expression as he climbs the main-skysail? Write a description of Buttons that you could give to the illustrator of the book jacket for *Redburn,* the book from which this excerpt is taken.

The River Took My Sister   (page 275)

1. Have you ever had something strange or unexpected happen to you in lovely surroundings on a beautiful day? Write a description of this event and of its setting. How will you describe the sharp contrast between the joyful mood of the setting and the unusual event itself?

2. In this poem and in "First Time Aloft," the authors express a similar tone, or attitude, about water. How is the tone of both pieces similar? Write a paragraph comparing the authors' tone in both pieces. Be sure to cite examples to support your opinion.

3. Why does the narrator return to the river, the scene of the tragedy? Pretend that you are the speaker. Write a letter to your mother explaining why you returned to the scene of the accident.

Sky Diver   (page 276)

1. Why is the speaker sky diving? Is the sky diver an adventurer or a person in the Air Force? Pretend that you are the sky diver. Do you feel excited? frightened? amazed? birdlike? Write a letter to a friend, explaining why you have undertaken this sport and how you feel when you are diving.

2. Write your interpretation of the last stanza of this poem. Defend your interpretation with reasons and examples from the poem.

3. What does the world below look like from the top of a mountain or a plane or a skyscraper or a Ferris wheel? Write a description about your view from one of these high places.

Prewriting Ideas: Description

Use these prewriting ideas to help you find topics to write about. After you have chosen a topic, use the activities to help you focus, explore, or narrow your topic.

- **Brainstorming objects**   Work with a small group taking turns. Very quickly name objects with which you are familiar. Then supply words to describe each object.

- **Brainstorming people**   Quickly list the names of people you could describe. Then list words that describe each person.

- **Brainstorming places**   Quickly list the names of places you have visited. Then list words to describe each place.

- **Brainstorming feelings**   List as quickly as you can feelings you remember. Quickly and briefly write notes to describe each feeling.

- **Free association**   Write the word *cheery, dreary, scary,* or *weary*. Then write the first word, phrase, or sentence that comes to mind. Keep writing until a description begins to take shape.

- **Sensory experiences**   Think of sights, sounds, smells, tastes, and textures you have experienced. Then choose one and describe it.

- **Talking and listening in pairs**   Choose a partner and describe an object or person to him or her. Then ask your partner to name the object or person. Reverse roles and repeat this process.

- **Show and tell**   Present an object to your classmates. Then ask them to describe it as completely as possible.

- **Taking notes**   Choose a subject you wish to describe. Research the topic by taking notes from reading or by observation. List details of how it looks, sounds, or behaves, and note special characteristics.

- **Looking at art**   Study paintings, photographs, or drawings. Use books, magazines, newspapers, or a trip to your local museum as resources. Describe, in notes or orally, what you see.

- **Listening to music**   Listen to a piece of music you like. Close your eyes and let the melody paint a picture for you. Then describe the people or scenes you imagined.

- **Dramatizing**   Pretend to be a character in a play. Act out a scene. Then have your classmates describe the kind of person you are.

- **Observing**   Study carefully a flower, insect, animal, or fountain. Then write notes of how it looks, sounds, behaves, or changes.

EXACTLY!

Objective
To use exact nouns, verbs, adjectives, and adverbs

Players
Any even number, divided into 1–5 pairs

You will need
30 index cards; a scorecard (on the next page); a thesaurus or a dictionary

Before you play
1. Write each of the following general nouns, verbs, adjectives, and adverbs on an index card: *chair, trip, big, bright, catch, eat, fast, funny, go, walk, good, happy, hot, move, mad, make, building, nice, quietly, run, say, start, rich, wrong, group, boat, water, land, picture, slowly.*
2. Choose 2 judges to rule on challenged words. (Sample answers are on the next page.)

How to play
1. Judges shuffle the word cards and place 6 cards face down in a pile between each pair of players.
2. The first player in each pair draws a card from the top of the pile and names as many exact words as possible for the general word. For example, a player who draws *sit* might say such words as *perch, recline, squat, plop, slump, sprawl.*
3. His or her opponent may challenge any words that are not exact words and may name other exact words. The judges use a thesaurus or a dictionary to decide if a challenged word will be accepted.
4. Players alternate drawing a card from the deck and naming as many exact words as possible.
5. Play continues for a specified time or until all the cards have been drawn.

Scoring
Players earn 1 point for each exact word they name. The player with the most points is the winner.

Variation
Instead of using the prepared list of words, Player 1 may select his or her own general word and challenge Player 2 to name exact words. If Player 2 cannot name any exact words, he or she returns the challenge to Player 1. If Player 1 cannot name an exact word, a point is deducted from his or her score.

Use with Composition Skills lesson, Descriptive Language, p. 285.

EXACTLY!

gloomy miserable **SAD** *forlorn downcast somber*

yell wail weep **CRY** *shout sob scream*

glance peek gawk **LOOK** *gaze stare gape*

Scorecard for each pair of players   Player 1   Player 2

	General Word	Player 1	Player 2
1			
2			
3			
4			
5			
6			
	Total Points		

Possible answers:

General Word	Possible answers	General Word	Possible answers
chair	rocker, stool, throne	make	construct, build, create
trip	journey, flight, voyage; tumble, sprawl, stumble	building	skyscraper, igloo, cabin
big	huge, gigantic, enormous	nice	polite, tasteful, kind
bright	luminous, vivid, brilliant	quietly	calmly, soundlessly, meekly
catch	hook, overtake, capture	run	scurry, flee, sprint
eat	consume, gobble, devour	say	announce, whisper, express
fast	swift, speedy, rapid	start	originate, lead, begin
funny	hilarious, witty, whimsical	rich	abundant, wealthy, elegant
go	travel, depart, wander	wrong	unjust, faulty, mistaken
walk	plod, hike, march	group	company, bunch, crowd
good	excellent, delicious, perfect	boat	yacht, canoe, submarine
happy	ecstatic, joyous, cheerful	water	ocean, lake, stream
hot	sweaty, boiling, sweltering	land	terrain, soil, country
move	leap, bolt, hop, jump	picture	photograph, painting, sketch
mad	furious, indignant, irritated	slowly	leisurely, gradually, pokily

Writing a Description • I

Directions: Imagine that you are inventing a new food to be used by astronauts during flight. The only requirements for the food are that it be healthful, compact, and appealing. What does your food look like? How does it taste, feel, and smell? Write a description of your new space food. Share your description with your friends.

Remember to

- choose details that create the overall impression you want to give
- organize your details
- use figurative language—similes and metaphors that compare the food or its qualities to other things or qualities
- use exact nouns, verbs, adjectives, and adverbs

Writing a Description • II

Directions: Imagine that you are inside this very old castle. What do you see? Is the atmosphere cheerful, bright, and airy? frightening, dark, and gloomy? Can you see clearly beyond the room you are in? What is on the other side of the walls of the room? Write a description of this castle for your classmates to read.

Remember to

- choose details that help create the overall impression you want to give
- organize your details
- use exact nouns, verbs, adjectives, and adverbs
- use descriptive language that makes comparisons

Name _____   Date _____

Planning a Description • I

What will you describe? What details will you include to create a sharp mental image of your topic? What exact words will you use to describe how your topic looks, sounds, feels, smells, and tastes?

Topic: _____

Details: _____

_____

_____

_____

_____

_____

_____

Exact words:

Looks	Sounds	Feels	Smells	Tastes

Name _____ Date _____

Planning a Description • II

Write your topic in the center of this page. Around it, write the different parts of the thing you are describing. Off each of these parts, write words to describe that part.

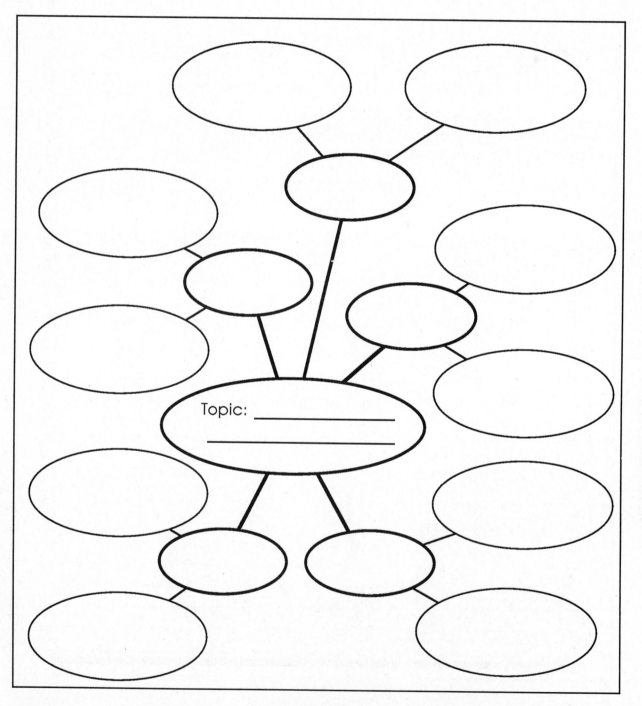

Topic: _____

The Writing Process, Step 1: Ideas for Getting Started, p. 291, "Cluster"

Writing a Description

Revising ☑

Did I use as many of my five senses as I could? ☐

Did I organize my details? ☐

Have I given my reader a clear picture of what I am talking about? ☐

Did I use figurative language or exact words where appropriate? ☐

Proofreading

Did I indent where necessary? ☐

Did I use capitals correctly? ☐

Did I punctuate correctly? ☐

Did I use adjectives and adverbs correctly? ☐

Did I spell all words correctly? ☐

Final Copy

Is my copy neat and accurate? ☐

Is my handwriting easy to read? ☐

Did I capitalize my title correctly? ☐

Did I leave proper space for margins? ☐

Did I skip a line after my title? ☐

Unit 8 • Self-evaluation Master

Your name _____   Writer's name _____

Writing a Description

Questions ☑	Comments
1. Where could the senses be used?	
2. Are details organized?	
3. Is there a clear picture of the subject?	
4. Where could figurative language and exact words be used?	

Student's name _____ Date _____

Description: Analytic Scale

	poor	weak	good	very good	excellent
Revising Skills ☑					
Five senses used	___	___	___	___	___
Details are organized	___	___	___	___	___
Clear picture of the subject	___	___	___	___	___
Figurative language or exact words used	___	___	___	___	___
Proofreading Skills					
Paragraphs indented	___	___	___	___	___
Capitals used correctly	___	___	___	___	___
Punctuation used correctly	___	___	___	___	___
Adjectives and adverbs used correctly	___	___	___	___	___
Words spelled correctly	___	___	___	___	___
Final Copy Skills					
Neat and accurate	___	___	___	___	___
Easy to read	___	___	___	___	___
Title capitalized correctly	___	___	___	___	___
Margins properly spaced	___	___	___	___	___
Title followed by line of space	___	___	___	___	___

Comments:

Total score _____

Letter grade
or percent _____

Unit 8 • Teacher Evaluation Master

Conversion Table

Scores	Letter Grade	Percent*
97–100	A+	_____
94–96	A	_____
90–93	A–	_____
83–89	B+	_____
77–82	B	_____
70–76	B–	_____
63-69	C+	_____
57–62	C	_____
50–56	C–	_____
43–49	D+	_____
37–42	D	_____
30–36	D–	_____
20–29	F	_____

*After you use the table to determine the letter grade, you can use your own school's system for reporting the percent that matches the letter grade.

Houghton Mifflin
English

LEVEL 8

Dear Parent,

Your child's English class is beginning a unit in HOUGHTON MIFFLIN ENGLISH called "Capitalization and Punctuation." In this unit, your child will practice writing, using the correct capitalization and end marks. Your child will learn that how a person punctuates a sentence affects a reader's or a listener's interpretation of what is being discussed.

To reinforce the skills in this unit, you may wish to do the following activity with your child.

Family Activity

- Read some newspaper headlines with your child. Together, change these headlines into sentences. How would you capitalize and punctuate them? Decide together.

If you have any questions about the skills or activities covered in this unit, please feel free to contact me.

Sincerely,

Unit 9 • Parent Letter

Estimado padre o madre,

La clase de inglés de su hijo o hija comienza una unidad en HOUGHTON MIFFLIN ENGLISH titulada *Capitalization and punctuation (El uso de las mayúsculas y de la puntuación).* En esta unidad, su hijo o hija practicará escribir usando las debidas letras mayúsculas y signos de puntuación. El o ella aprenderá que la manera en que uno usa la puntuación en una oración afecta también la interpretación del lector o de la persona que escucha, sobre lo que uno dice.

Para reforzar las destrezas de esta unidad, quizás le interese compartir la siguiente actividad con su hijo o hija.

Actividad para la familia

■ Lea algunos titulares de un periódico con su hijo o hija. Juntos, cambien estos titulares para formar oraciones. ¿Qué uso harían de las letras mayúsculas y de los signos de puntuación? Decidan juntos.

Si usted tiene alguna pregunta sobre las destrezas o actividades que se presentan en esta unidad, por favor sienta la libertad de comunicarse conmigo.

Sinceramente,

What's Missing .,:-"" !?;

Objective
To use punctuation marks correctly

Players
2–6

You will need
Six 2" × 12" tagboard strips (or at least 1 for each player); 54 triangular-shaped pieces of tagboard (pattern on the next page); a scorecard (on the next page); pens or pencils; sentences with punctuation marks omitted (sample sentences and answers on the next page)

Before you play
1. On each of the triangular-shaped cards, players write one of the following punctuation marks: 10 periods, 6 question marks, 4 exclamation points, 12 commas, 4 sets of quotation marks (1 set of beginning and ending quotes on each card), 4 colons, 4 semicolons, 8 apostrophes, and 2 dashes.
2. Choose a leader to write sentences. (He or she may use the samples on the next page.) Each sentence must contain at least 4 punctuation marks. The sentence should be copied onto a tagboard strip. The leader takes care to omit certain punctuation marks and does not leave unnatural spaces as clues to where the punctuation belongs.

How to play
1. The leader shuffles the punctuation cards and the sentence cards and deals 1 sentence card and 6 punctuation cards to each player.
2. Players place their sentence cards face up on the playing surface in front of them.
3. Players use their punctuation cards to punctuate the sentences. Example:

No I set the alarm for 5 15 A M

4. Players probably will need additional punctuation marks. Starting with the person to the right of the leader, each player draws one punctuation card from the deck and discards a card.
5. Play continues until a player punctuates his or her sentence.

Scoring
Players earn 1 point for each punctuation mark used correctly in their sentences. Any player can challenge another player's use of a punctuation mark. Players earn 1 point for each error they identify. The player with the most points is the winner.

What's Missing?

Sample sentences

1. We arrived in Rochester New York, on March 3 1990 at 5 30 PM.
2. Yes, I visited Butte Montana last fall replied Mrs Sacco.
3. Did Longfellow write the poem The Midnight Ride of Paul Revere or did the author Robert Frost
4. Please bring the following a notebook pencils a ruler an eraser and some reference books
5. Johns brother doesnt dot his is or cross his ts therefore his writing is often difficult to read

Punctuation cards

1. Triangles can be this size:
2. Distinguish commas from apostrophes this way:

   (comma)   (apostrophe)

Scorecard

PLAYERS' NAMES	POINTS		
	Punctuation Added Correctly	Errors Identified	Total

Houghton Mifflin English 8. Copyright © Houghton Mifflin Company. All rights reserved.

Unit 9 • Game

Answers
1. We arrived in Rochester, New York, on March 3, 1990, at 5:30 P.M.
2. "Yes, I visited Butte, Montana, last fall," replied Mrs. Sacco.
3. Did Longfellow write the poem "The Midnight Ride of Paul Revere," or did the author Robert Frost?
4. Please bring the following: a notebook, pencils, a ruler, an eraser, and some reference books.
5. John's brother doesn't dot his i's or cross his t's; therefore, his writing is often difficult to read.

140

Houghton Mifflin
English

LEVEL 8

Dear Parent,

Every day we encounter methods of persuasion—in advertisements, newspaper editorials, and political statements, for example. Even at home a tempting piece of food will draw forth a child's best persuasive talents! In this literature and writing unit of HOUGHTON MIFFLIN ENGLISH, your child will be introduced to various persuasive techniques to help him or her create a worthwhile argument. Your child will also learn how to write various kinds of letters. Finally he or she will write a persuasive letter, using the five steps of the writing process.

To help your child recognize propaganda techniques and use effective methods of persuasion, try one or more of the activities below.

Family Activities

- The next time your child asks your permission to do something, ask him or her these questions:
  1. Can you offer a precedent?
  2. Have you thought of why I might object? Can you respond to these objections?
  3. What could happen if you succeed in persuading me? Have you explored the consequences?
  4. If you are accusing me of being unfair, do you have a solid example to show why you should be given permission?

- After your child has selected a topic for his or her persuasive letter, discuss the topic. Take an opposing point of view, playing "devil's advocate."

If you have any questions or comments about the skills or activities in this unit, please do not hesitate to contact me.

Sincerely,

Unit 10 • Parent Letter

141

Houghton Mifflin
English

Estimado padre o madre,

Todos los días nos encontramos con diferentes métodos de persuasión, en los anuncios, en los editoriales de los periódicos, y en las declaraciones políticas, por ejemplo. Hasta en el hogar, una comida tentadora hará surgir los mejores talentos de persuasión de un niño. En esta unidad de literatura y redacción de HOUGHTON MIFFLIN ENGLISH, su hijo o hija conocerá varias técnicas de persuasión que le permitirán crear un argumento que valga la pena. El o ella también aprenderá cómo escribir varios tipos de carta, y finalmente redactará una carta de persuasión, siguiendo los cinco pasos del proceso de redacción.

Para ayudar a su hijo o hija a reconocer las técnicas de propaganda, prueben una o más de las siguientes actividades.

Actividades para la familia

- La próxima vez que su hijo o hija le pida permiso para hacer algo, hágale las siguientes preguntas:
  1. ¿Me puedes mencionar algún precedente?
  2. ¿Has pensado porqué yo me podría oponer? ¿Puedes refutarme estas objeciones?
  3. ¿Cuál podría ser el resultado si logras persuadirme? ¿Has explorado las consecuencias?
  4. Si me acusas de no ser justo, ¿tienes un buen ejemplo para demostrarme porqué deberías recibir permiso?

- Después de que su hijo o hija haya seleccionado los temas para su carta de persuasión, hablen sobre el tema. Tome el punto de vista contrario, jugando al "abogado del diablo."

Si usted tiene alguna pregunta o comentario sobre las destrezas o actividades de esta unidad, por favor no demore en comunicarse conmigo.

Sinceramente,

Writing About the Literature

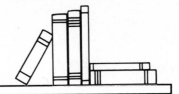

O Captain! My Captain! (page 346)

1. Write a poem about a person who is important to you. What symbol might you use to represent this person? Can you use repetition to emphasize your feelings?

2. Do you want to know more about the life of Lincoln? about Lincoln as President? about the Civil War? Write a research report about some aspect of American history at the time "O Captain! My Captain!" was written.

3. Whitman describes a particular crowd scene vividly. Pretend that you are a spectator in this crowd. What do you see? How do you feel? Write a description of the scene from a spectator's point of view.

4. How was Abraham Lincoln like a captain? Write one or two paragraphs comparing Lincoln to a ship's captain.

Lincoln's Reply (page 348)

1. Did Johnston take his stepbrother's advice? How did Lincoln's proposal work out? Write a dialogue that takes place ten years later between Johnston and Lincoln.

2. Do you need or want a loan? What for? How would you repay the loan? Write a letter to a relative. Convince him or her to lend you money for something you need or want.

3. Play devil's advocate. Imagine that you are Lincoln's friend, and you do not believe that he should lend Johnston the money. Write a letter to Lincoln giving reasons that support your opinion.

4. What was Johnston like? Write a description of him, using what you learn about him from Lincoln's letter.

5. Do you know anyone who seems like either Johnston or Lincoln? someone who is not lazy but an idler or someone who is generous and sympathetic? Write a paragraph comparing this person to Johnston or to Lincoln.

Prewriting Ideas: Persuasive Letter

Use these prewriting ideas to help you find topics to write about. After you have chosen a topic, use the activities to help you focus, explore, or narrow your topic.

- **Brainstorming opinions** Work with a small group. Quickly list ideas you have about social issues such as health care, conservation, or education. Discuss what people, organizations, and governments can do about those issues.

- **Talking and listening in groups** Tell the group how you would solve a problem in your school, neighborhood, town, city, state, or country. Then listen to their ideas for solutions to the problem.

- **Debating** Choose two classmates for your debating team, and three classmates as the opposition. Debate a common problem and propose a solution. Then let the opposition propose a different solution and argue against your solution.

- **Discussion** Pretend that your class is at a conference. Circulate from person to person, discussing possible solutions to serious problems that face people today.

- **Panel discussions** Form a panel of classroom "experts" who have knowledge or experience of a problem. Then let the panel speak to the class and answer questions.

- **Role-playing** Pretend to be a person who is seeking help with a problem. Select classmates to represent organizations and individuals who may have a solution to the problem. Then act out one solution to the problem.

- **Observing** Look around your community or state. Note improvements that are needed. Tell how people can make those improvements.

- **Listing** List habits that are unwise or unhealthy. Then note reasons to avoid such activities and present ideas for prevention.

- **Taking notes** Take notes of problems that you see, hear, or read about. Note solutions that have been proposed for those problems. Give your opinion of which solutions would work and explain why.

- **Reading magazines, books, newspapers** Discover ways that people have solved problems. Note whether their solutions would work for other people, and tell why you think this.

- **Improvising** Work with the entire class or a small group. The teacher or a designated student will give you a "problem." List solutions to the problem that come from your group.

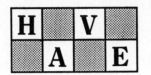 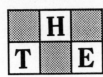 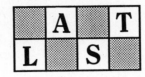 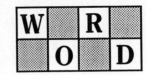

Objective
To use persuasive strategies

Players
2, and a judge

You will need
Index cards; red and white construction paper; a game board (on the next page)

Before you play
1. Cut 4 red and 4 white circles 1″ wide; these will be game markers. Write these 4 strategies on each set of circles: *Offer a precedent, Appeal to fairness, Overcome objections,* and *Explore consequences.*
2. Brainstorm a list of proposals, or use the samples on the next page.
3. Write each proposal in question form on an index card. Shuffle the cards, and place them face down in a pile.
4. Choose 1 or 2 judges to make decisions when players challenge each other. NOTE: The judges and players may want to reread the explanation of the strategies on page 363 of your *Houghton Mifflin English* textbook.

How to play
1. Each player chooses a set of red or white game markers and places them on a star row of the game board. Either player turns up the top question card.
2. In order to move markers, the red-marker player must give a reason why a proposal *should* be adopted and the white-marker player must tell why it *should not* be adopted. For example, suppose the question is, *Should all students study a foreign language?* If the red player decides to move the *Offer a precedent* marker, he or she might say, "Yes. In Sweden, where a second language is required, many people speak both Swedish and English and have more job opportunities."
3. As in checkers, players take turns moving the markers forward *diagonally*, one square at a time. The markers cannot be moved backward.
4. Any player who uses the wrong strategy or cannot think of a reason must not move the marker.
5. After each player has had a chance to move all 4 markers, a new question card is turned over.
6. As in checkers, a player may capture his or her opponent's marker by jumping over it.
7. When a player's marker reaches the other side of the board, it is crowned "king." The other player places a captured marker on top. The king can move forward *and* backward, but only diagonally.
8. The winner is the player who blocks or captures all of the opponent's markers, so that the opponent can no longer move.

Use with Composition Skills lesson, Using Persuasive Strategies, p. 363.

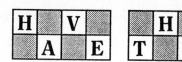 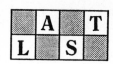 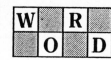

HAVE THE LAST WORD

Sample questions

1. Should all students be required to participate in a team sport?
2. Should schools be open for twelve months?
3. Should the speed limit on all highways be raised to 65 mph?
4. Should gasoline-powered vehicles be banned by the year 2000?
5. Should physical education class be required every semester?

Game board

Writing a Persuasive Letter • I

Directions: Your school is thinking about an Artists-in-the-Schools program. This program would involve an artist visiting your school three days a week for one month. Each class would meet with the artist for a half day during the month. Each month a different kind of artist would visit.

The principal has asked students and teachers to write letters expressing their opinions about this program. Decide whether you are for or against the program. Think of several strong reasons to support your opinion. Then write a persuasive letter to the principal.

Remember to

- follow correct business letter style and form
- state your opinion clearly and give reasons and examples that support it
- use persuasive strategies
- organize your reasons and examples from most-to-least or from least-to-most important

Writing a Persuasive Letter • II

Directions: Pretend that you are the owner of a vacation resort. You have found out that a large group from another state is planning a group vacation at a resort, and you want them to come to yours. Why would your resort appeal to this group? What sports do you offer? What is the setting like? What kind of food do you serve? Write a letter to persuade this group to stay at your resort.

Remember to

- follow correct business letter style and form
- state your opinion clearly and give reasons and examples that support it
- use persuasive strategies
- organize your reasons and examples from most-to-least or from least-to-most important

Unit 10 • Writing Prompts

Planning a Persuasive Letter • I

Pretend that you are a defense lawyer, and you must present your argument as
well as overcome the objections of your opponent, the prosecuting lawyer. Fill
in the plan below.

Who: *(Whom must you convince?)* _____

What: *(What must you convince them of?)* _____

_____

Why: *(What do you hope to gain?)* _____

_____

Possible objections: How I will overcome objections:

Unit 10 • Prewriting Master

Planning a Persuasive Letter • II

Plan your letter. First write your opinion.

_____

_____

_____

Next, brainstorm, writing everything you can think of about your argument.

_____

_____

_____

_____

_____

_____

_____

_____

Now cross out the reasons from above that are not relevant or specific.
On the lines below, list your reasons in order.

_____

_____

_____

_____

_____

The Writing Process, Step 1: Ideas for Getting Started, p. 367, "Chart It"

Writing a Persuasive Letter

Revising ☑

Did I state my opinion clearly? ☐

Did I support my opinion with relevant reasons and factual examples? ☐

Are my reasons ordered effectively? ☐

Does each paragraph have a topic sentence? ☐

Is my purpose clear? ☐

Did I use all possible persuasive strategies? ☐

Proofreading

Did I follow proper business letter form? ☐

Did I capitalize correctly? ☐

Did I punctuate properly? ☐

Did I use abbreviations and numbers correctly? ☐

Did I spell all words correctly? ☐

Final Copy

Is my copy neat and accurate? ☐

Is my handwriting easy to read? ☐

Is my title capitalized correctly? ☐

Did I leave proper space for margins? ☐

Did I skip a line after my title? ☐

Unit 10 • Self-evaluation Master

The Writing Process, Steps 3, 4, 5

Your name _____ Writer's name _____

Writing a Persuasive Letter

Questions ☑	Comments
1. Is the opinion stated clearly?	
2. Where could opinions be supported with more reasons and factual examples?	
3. Are the reasons organized effectively?	
4. Does each paragraph have a topic sentence?	
5. Is the writer's purpose clear?	

The Writing Process, Step 3: Revise

Student's name _____ Date _____

Persuasive Letter: Analytic Scale

	poor	weak	good	very good	excellent
Revising Skills ☑					
Opinion stated clearly	——	——	——	——	——
Reasons and facts support opinion	——	——	——	——	——
Reasons ordered effectively	——	——	——	——	——
Topic sentence for each paragraph	——	——	——	——	——
Purpose is clear	——	——	——	——	——
Persuasive strategies used	——	——	——	——	——
Proofreading Skills					
Proper business letter form	——	——	——	——	——
Capitals used correctly	——	——	——	——	——
Punctuation used correctly	——	——	——	——	——
Abbreviations and numbers used correctly	——	——	——	——	——
Words spelled correctly	——	——	——	——	——
Final Copy Skills					
Neat and accurate	——	——	——	——	——
Easy to read	——	——	——	——	——
Title capitalized correctly	——	——	——	——	——
Margins properly spaced	——	——	——	——	——
Title followed by line of space	——	——	——	——	——

Comments:

Total score _____

Letter grade
or percent _____

Unit 10 • Teacher Evaluation Master

The Conversion Table on the next page will help you with scoring.
The Writing Process, Steps 3, 4, 5

Conversion Table

Scores	Letter Grade	Percent*
97–100	A+	_____
94–96	A	_____
90–93	A–	_____
83–89	B+	_____
77–82	B	_____
70–76	B–	_____
63-69	C+	_____
57–62	C	_____
50–56	C–	_____
43–49	D+	_____
37–42	D	_____
30–36	D–	_____
20–29	F	_____

*After you use the table to determine the letter grade, you can use your own school's system for reporting the percent that matches the letter grade.

Houghton Mifflin
English

LEVEL 8

Dear Parent,

Your child is beginning a language and usage unit in HOUGHTON MIFFLIN ENGLISH called "Pronouns." Your child will learn about various kinds of pronouns and how to use their different forms correctly. Throughout this unit, your child will learn to use pronouns to make his or her writing smooth, clear, and correct.

Try one or more of the activities below to help reinforce some of the skills your child learns in this unit.

Family Activities

- Look at some family photographs. Have your child make up questions that an outsider might ask. Ask your child to use interrogative pronouns (for example, ***Who****'s that?* ***Whose*** *is that? With* ***whom*** *are you talking?*).

- The next time your child uses unclear pronouns (such as ***They*** *say* ***you*** *aren't allowed to chew gum),* ask him or her to reword the sentence to clarify the pronouns (for example, ***The teacher*** *says* ***students*** *aren't allowed to chew gum).*

Please feel free to contact me if you have any questions about the skills and activities presented in this unit.

Sincerely,

Unit 11 • Parent Letter

Estimado padre o madre,

Su hijo o hija comienza una unidad de gramática en HOUGHTON MIFFLIN ENGLISH titulada *Pronouns (Los pronombres).* El o ella aprenderá sobre varios tipos de pronombre y cómo usar correctamente las diferentes formas. En toda esta unidad, su hijo o hija aprenderá a usar los pronombres para escribir con fluidez, claridad y corrección.

Pruebe una o más de las siguientes actividades para ayudar a reforzar algunas de las destrezas que aprende su hijo o hija en esta unidad.

Actividades para la familia

- Examinen algunas fotos de la familia. Pídale a su hijo o hija que formule preguntas que podría hacer alguien que no los conoce. Pídale que use pronombres interrogativos, como *Who's that? (¿Quién es ese?), Whose is that? (¿De quién es eso?),* y *With whom are you talking? (¿Con quién habla?).*

- La próxima vez que su hijo o hija use pronombres que no sean claros, como en la oración *They say you aren't allowed to chew gum (Dicen que no se permite masticar chicle),* pídale que cambie las palabras de la oración para clarificar los pronombres (por ejemplo: *The teacher says students aren't allowed to chew gum —El maestro dice que a los estudiantes no se les permite masticar chicle).*

Por favor sienta la libertad de comunicarse conmigo si tiene alguna pregunta sobre las destrezas o actividades que se presentan en esta unidad.

Sinceramente,

Proverbs and PRONOUNS

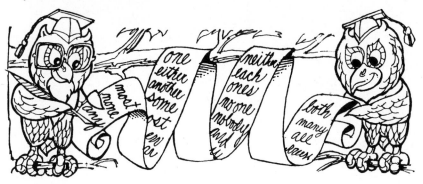

Objective
To identify indefinite pronouns

Players
Any number, divided into 2 teams

You will need
Index cards; 18 scrambled proverbs and answers (on the next page); a timer; pencils and paper

Before you play
1. Choose a leader who will prepare the proverb cards by cutting out and mounting the scrambled statements on index cards.
2. The leader shuffles the cards and places them face down between the 2 teams.
3. Choose a timekeeper who is also the scorekeeper.

How to play
1. The first player on Team A draws a card and has 1 minute to unscramble the proverb (a well-known saying) written on the card. The player must also identify the indefinite pronoun in the proverb. The leader checks the proverb and the pronoun with the answers on the next page.
2. Players alternate drawing cards from the deck, with the first player on Team A followed by the first player on Team B. If a player cannot unscramble a proverb, a player on the opposing team is given a chance to unscramble it. That team may then have its regular turn.
3. The game is over when all the proverb cards have been drawn.

Scoring
A player earns 1 point for every correctly unscrambled proverb and 1 point for each indefinite pronoun that is correctly identified. The team with the most points is the winner.

Variations
- Both teams are given a list of proverbs to unscramble within a specified time limit. The team that unscrambles the most proverbs and correctly identifies the indefinite pronouns is the winner.

Use with Lesson 6, Indefinite Pronouns, p. 393.

Proverbs and PRONOUNS

Sample scrambled proverbs

1. ventured nothing nothing gained
2. his to own each
3. is vanity all
4. not that all glitters gold is
5. for place everything in everything place its a and
6. nothing doing is everything doing
7. can't start you finish don't anything
8. comes who him waits everything to
9. conquers all conquers he himself who
10. the come will wash all it in out
11. a fool crown wore every if, all should we kings be
12. are called many are few but chosen
13. would you others them do you unto as have do unto
14. wise some are, otherwise some and are
15. new the there's under nothing sun
16. goes everyone grass grows never where
17. so bad it could there but be worse is nothing what
18. well well that all's ends

Answers

NOTE: *Indefinite pronouns are underlined.*
Some proverbs, such as 3 below, can be correctly unscrambled in more than 1 way and still have the same meaning.

1. Nothing ventured, nothing <u>gained</u>.
2. To <u>each</u> his own.
3. <u>All</u> is vanity, or Vanity is <u>all</u>.
4. <u>All</u> that glitters is not gold.
5. A place for <u>everything</u>, and <u>everything</u> in its place.
6. Doing <u>everything</u> is doing <u>nothing</u>.
7. Don't start <u>anything</u> you can't finish.
8. <u>Everything</u> comes to him who waits.
9. He who conquers himself conquers all.
10. It will <u>all</u> come out in the wash.
11. If every fool wore a crown, we should all be kings.
12. <u>Many</u> are called, but few are chosen.
13. Do unto <u>others</u> as you would have them do unto you.
14. <u>Some</u> are wise, and <u>some</u> are otherwise.
15. There's <u>nothing</u> new under the sun.
16. Where <u>everyone</u> goes grass grows.
17. There is <u>nothing</u> so bad but what it could be worse.
18. <u>All's</u> well that ends well.

Houghton Mifflin
English

LEVEL 8

Dear Parent,

Throughout his or her school career as well as in everyday life, your child uses reference materials as tools to answer questions of fact—to find out a team's score or to write a school report, for example. In this literature and writing unit of HOUGHTON MIFFLIN ENGLISH, your child will learn more about various reference aids and will use them to write a short research report. Following the steps of the writing process, your child will choose and narrow a topic, plan and research the report, write the first draft, revise its content, proofread it for errors, and make a final copy to share with classmates.

You may wish to try one of the following activities to help your child practice finding facts.

Family Activities

- Let your child take responsibility for finding factual information such as the weather, a sports score, and other questions of fact that arise.

- If your family is planning a vacation or a visit to a tourist attraction, let your child take part in making the plans. He or she might research the site, finally serving as the family's guide once you are underway.

If you have any questions about the skills and activities in this unit, please feel free to contact me.

Sincerely,

Unit 12 • Parent Letter

Estimado padre o madre,

Durante su carrera académica como también en la vida cotidiana, su hijo o hija usa materiales de referencia como recursos para contestar preguntas sobre hechos—para descubrir la anotación de un equipo, por ejemplo, o para redactar un informe para la escuela. En esta unidad de literatura y redacción de HOUGHTON MIFFLIN ENGLISH, su hijo o hija aprenderá más sobre los diferentes recursos de referencia y los utilizará para escribir un breve informe de investigación. Primero, su hijo o hija aprenderá a evaluar la información, a escoger un tema, y a planificar e investigar el informe tomando apuntes y haciendo un bosquejo. Finalmente, siguiendo los pasos del proceso de redacción, él o ella escogerá un tema que reducirá, planificará e investigará el tema, escribirá el primer borrador, revisará el contenido, le corregirá los errores, y hará una copia final en limpio para compartirla con los compañeros de clase.

Quizás le interese a usted probar una de las siguientes actividades para ayudar a su hijo o hija a encontrar datos.

Actividades para la familia

- Permita que su hijo o hija asuma responsabilidad por encontrar datos informativos como el estado del tiempo, los resultados de una competencia deportiva, u otras preguntas que puedan surgir sobre datos.

- Si la familia planifica tomar una vacación o visitar alguna atracción turística, permita que su hijo o hija participe en los planes. El o ella podría investigar el lugar, sirviendo como el guía de la familia una vez salgan de camino.

Si usted tiene preguntas sobre las destrezas o actividades de esta unidad, por favor sienta la libertad de comunicarse conmigo.

Sinceramente,

Writing About the Literature

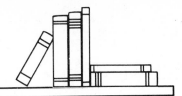

Geography Lesson   (page 418)

1. Imagine that you are the speaker in the poem and you are still in the jet. As the jet descends, your geography lesson continues. Write one or two more stanzas of the poem, illustrating what you learn.

2. Write a story with the speaker of this poem as the main character. Create your plot around the conflict between this character, who cannot understand people's hatred, and another character, who does understand people's hatred.

3. Imagine that you know the speaker well and you are writing a letter to recommend him or her for a job. Since this job involves working closely with people, you will want to write about your friend's personal qualities. Who is the speaker? How old is he or she? What does he or she do now for a living? What is his or her attitude toward people? Do you admire this person? Write your letter to persuade an employer to hire your friend.

The Eagle   (page 420)

1. Using Tennyson's poem as a model, write your own poem about a different bird. Can you use alliteration to fit your subject?

2. Imagine that you wrote this poem. Where were you when you wrote it? What moved you to write it? What were you trying to accomplish? Write your diary entry, describing your experience while you wrote the poem.

3. What is the eagle thinking about the world below? Are its thoughts majestic? What does it see? Pretend to be the eagle. Write a description of what you see and what you are thinking.

Early Theories of Flight   (page 421)

1. Write a research report about the history of heavier-than-air or lighter-than-air machines.

2. Imagine what it is like to spend eight to ten hours in an airplane in flight. Do you learn a lot about another passenger? Do you feel the need to move around? Write a story in which the setting is an airplane during a long flight.

3. How is a train like an airplane? How are these two methods of transportation different? Write a composition in which you compare and contrast any two means of travel.

Prewriting Ideas: Research Report

Use these prewriting ideas to help you find topics to write about. After you have chosen a topic, use the activities to help you focus, explore, or narrow your topic.

- **Reading books, magazines, newspapers** Look through printed materials for interesting articles and ideas. Note fashions, inventions, trends, and ideas you would like to know more about. Then make a list of information you would like to obtain about one of those topics.

- **Watching television** List shows, actors, and ideas you have seen that interest you. Choose one and note questions you have about that topic.

- **Interest inventory** List things that interest you: hobbies, sports, games, art, music, politics. Choose one topic to research. List information you will need to find.

- **Brainstorming** Write the name of an idea, process, person, place, or thing that interests you. As quickly as possible, write what you know about that subject. Then quickly list questions you have on your topic.

- **Talking and listening in groups** Take turns telling about an interesting topic. Encourage listeners to ask questions about it.

- **Discussion** Set aside class time for an informal get-together. Circulate around the room, talking to various classmates. Discuss the topics you would like to research for a report.

- **Panel discussions** Form a panel of five or six classmates. Have the panel discuss a topic of interest to the class. Then question the panelists for more information.

- **Show and tell** Bring to class an object or picture of something about which you would like to write a research report. Then tell the class the information you plan to present in your report.

- **Observing** Look around your classroom, neighborhood, or home to find ideas for report topics. Note things, activities, and ideas you could report on. Choose one topic and write questions you would like answered about it.

- **Outlining** Write down the topic you would like to research. Below it, write in outline form the main and sub-points you will cover.

- **Looking at art** Study paintings, sculpture, drawings, or photographs. List what you would like to know about the artist, photographer, or subject depicted. Then note where you might find that information.

Furthermore...

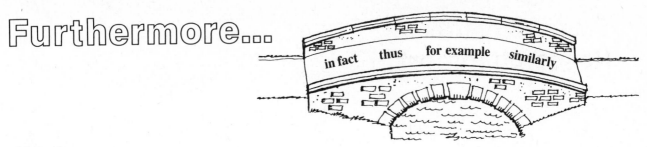

in fact   thus   for example   similarly

Objective

To use transitional words and phrases in research-report situations

Players

Any number, divided into 2 teams

You will need

Reference sources—encyclopedia, atlas, almanac, dictionary; 2 sets of 12 index cards, each set a different color; a timer; a scorecard (on the next page)

Before you play

On 1 set of cards, write 1 of the following purposes for using a transitional phrase: *Introduce an example, Add another point, Show a time relationship, Signal a result or an effect, Show comparison or contrast,* and *Connect ideas.* Include examples of appropriate transitional words and phrases for each purpose (refer to page 443 of your Houghton Mifflin English textbook). Do this twice. On each card of the other set, write a sentence that could be an introduction to a research report (sample sentences on the next page). Choose a leader and a scorekeeper.

How to play

1. The leader shuffles the transition cards and the introduction cards and places them face down in 2 piles. Then he or she draws an introduction card and reads the topic aloud.
2. The first player on Team A draws a card from the transition deck and, within a specified time (such as 3 minutes), must add a statement that begins with the selected transition. (Reference aids may be used.) For example, if the introductory statement is *Many animals have become extinct,* a player who draws an *Introduce an example* card might say, "For example, mammoths died off thousands of years ago."
3. Then the first player on Team B draws a card from the transition deck and adds a new statement. For example, if the player draws a *Show comparison or contrast* card, he or she might say, "Similarly, the saber-toothed tiger has been extinct since the Ice Age."
4. If the transitional statement is challenged, the leader decides whether or not to award points.
5. Players on the 2 teams take turns until 2 players in a row are unable to add a statement or until all 12 transition cards have been drawn. The leader draws a new introduction card, and the game continues until all the introduction cards have been drawn.

Scoring

For each statement, players earn 2 points. The team with the most points wins.

Use with Composition Skills lesson, Making Transitions, p. 442.

Unit 12 • Game

163

Furthermore...

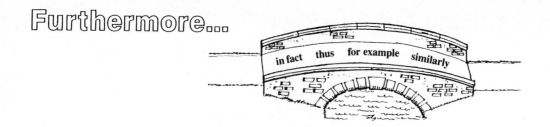

in fact thus for example similarly

Sample introductory statements

- In years to come, the twentieth century may be known as the Age of Communication.
- The planets in our solar system are all very different.
- Different plants grow in different parts of the world.
- Some animals are vertebrates, and some animals are invertebrates.
- Throughout history people have invented devices to meet the needs of society.
- Baseball is still a popular sport.
- Movies are a mirror of society.
- Television is an important educational tool.
- Rock and country are two of the most popular types of music today.

Scorecard

	TEAM A	TEAM B
Introductory Statement		
Number of Added Statements		
Total Points		
Introductory Statement		
Number of Added Statements		
Total Points		
Grand Total		

Unit 12 • Game

Writing a Research Report • I

Directions: Write a research report about your state capital. Why was this city chosen as the state capital? Why is the city interesting to visit? What sights does it offer to tourists? Who designed the capitol building? When was it built? You may need to narrow your topic to the history of the capital city or to tourist attractions. Let your classmates learn about your capital by reading your report.

Remember to

- take notes
- make an outline
- write an attention-getting introduction
- write a conclusion that summarizes the main points
- use transition words

Writing a Research Report • II

Directions: What is your favorite holiday? Why is it celebrated? Where and when was it first celebrated? Whom does it honor? Write a factual report for your classmates to learn about the history of your favorite holiday.

Remember to

- take notes
- make an outline
- write an attention-getting introduction
- write a conclusion that summarizes the main points
- use transition words

Planning a Research Report • I

I am going to write about _____

My beginning should capture a reader's interest. A brief story or anecdote that I might tell is _____

_____

_____

_____

_____

_____

My beginning should also include a sentence that tells what the report is about. Here is a sentence I

could use in my beginning. _____

_____

_____

My conclusion should restate the main idea of my report and review the main points. Here is one

way that I could end my report. _____

_____

_____

_____

_____

_____

_____

Unit 12 • Prewriting Master

Planning a Research Report • II

My report will be about _____

Here are the questions I want to answer in my report.

_____

_____

_____

_____

_____

Research the answers to your questions. Write the information on note cards. Did you add or change any questions as you did your research? Write any new or different questions here.

_____

_____

_____

_____

Now write your questions as main topics for your outline. Write your main topics below. Think about the best order for your main topics.

I. _____

II. _____

III. _____

IV. _____

V. _____

Now write your complete outline on another piece of paper. Write the main topics you listed above. Write the facts on your note cards as the subtopics and details under the main topics.

The Writing Process, Step 1: Ideas for Getting Started, p. 447, "Writing Questions"

Writing a Research Report

Revising ☑

Did I introduce my topic in an interesting way? ☐
Is the information complete and clearly presented? ☐
Does each paragraph focus on one main idea? ☐
Does each paragraph lead logically to the next? ☐
Does the conclusion summarize the main ideas? ☐

Proofreading

Did I indent paragraphs and sources? ☐
Did I spell all words correctly? ☐
Did I capitalize and punctuate correctly? ☐
Did I use commas correctly? ☐
Did I use the correct forms of nouns and pronouns? ☐

Final Copy

Is my copy neat and accurate? ☐
Is my handwriting easy to read? ☐
Did I capitalize my title correctly? ☐
Did I leave proper space for margins? ☐
Did I skip a line after my title? ☐

Unit 12 • Self-evaluation Master

Your name _____

Writer's name _____

Writing a Research Report

Questions ☑	Comments
1. Is the topic introduced in an interesting way?	
2. Is the information complete and clearly presented?	
3. Does each paragraph focus on one main idea?	
4. Where could transitions between paragraphs be added?	
5. Does the conclusion summarize the main ideas?	

Student's name _____ Date _____

Research Report: Analytic Scale

	poor	weak	good	very good	excellent
Revising Skills ☑					
Interesting introduction	____	____	____	____	____
Complete and clear information	____	____	____	____	____
One main idea per paragraph	____	____	____	____	____
Logical transitions between paragraphs	____	____	____	____	____
Main ideas summarized in conclusion	____	____	____	____	____
Proofreading Skills					
Paragraphs and sources are indented	____	____	____	____	____
Words spelled correctly	____	____	____	____	____
Capitals and punctuation used correctly	____	____	____	____	____
Commas used correctly	____	____	____	____	____
Correct forms of nouns and pronouns	____	____	____	____	____
Final Copy Skills					
Neat and accurate	____	____	____	____	____
Easy to read	____	____	____	____	____
Title capitalized correctly	____	____	____	____	____
Margins properly spaced	____	____	____	____	____
Title followed by line of space	____	____	____	____	____

Comments:

Total score _____

Letter grade
or percent _____

Unit 12 • Teacher Evaluation Master

Conversion Table

Scores	Letter Grade	Percent*
97–100	A+	_____
94–96	A	_____
90–93	A–	_____
83–89	B+	_____
77–82	B	_____
70–76	B–	_____
63–69	C+	_____
57–62	C	_____
50–56	C–	_____
43–49	D+	_____
37–42	D	_____
30–36	D–	_____
20–29	F	_____

*After you use the table to determine the letter grade, you can use your own school's system for reporting the percent that matches the letter grade.

Houghton Mifflin
English

LEVEL 8

Dear Parent,

Your child is beginning a language and usage unit in HOUGHTON MIFFLIN ENGLISH called "Phrases." In this unit, your child will identify different kinds of phrases and write better sentences with clear modifying phrases.

To help your child place phrases so that they refer clearly to the words they modify, you may wish to try the activity below.

Family Activity

- Make up headlines for imaginary newspaper articles about members of your family. These headlines can be humorous and should have misplaced phrases (for example, *Teen Sees Empire State Building on Vacation*). Have your child restate the headlines, placing the phrases correctly. Your child may enjoy making up his or her own headlines and trying them out on you!

If you have any questions about this unit, please feel free to contact me.

Sincerely,

Unit 13 • Parent Letter

Estimado padre o madre,

Su hijo o hija comienza una unidad de gramática en HOUGHTON MIFFLIN ENGLISH que se titula *Phrases (Las frases).* En esta unidad, él o ella identificará diferentes tipos de frases y redactará oraciones mejor escritas, usando frases modificadoras claras.

Para ayudar a que su hijo o hija pueda colocar las frases de manera que se refieran claramente a las palabras que modifican, a usted quizás le interese probar la siguiente actividad.

Actividad para la familia

- Inventen titulares para artículos imaginarios de un periódico sobre la familia. Estos titulares podrían ser cómicos, y deberán tener frases colocadas incorrectamente, por ejemplo, *Teen Sees Empire State Building on Vacation.* Pídale a su hijo o hija que vuelva a formular los titulares, colocando correctamente las frases. ¡Quizás él o ella disfrute de crear sus propios titulares y decírselos a usted!

Si tiene alguna pregunta sobre esta unidad, por favor sienta la libertad de comunicarse conmigo.

Sinceramente,

Verbal Race Track

Objective
To use verbals—participles, gerunds, and infinitives—in sentences

Players
2–5

You will need
A game board and a spinner (on the next page); an arrow for the spinner; a rivet or paper fastener to attach the arrow; 7 index cards, cut in half (fourteen $1\frac{1}{2}'' \times 2\frac{1}{2}''$ cards); buttons for game markers; paper and pencil for each player

Before you play
Choose a leader to write the following words and phrases on the 14 cards: *participle* on 4 cards; 1 card each for *gerund—subject*, *gerund—direct object*, *gerund—object of preposition*, *gerund—predicate noun*, *infinitive—noun (subject)*, *infinitive—noun (direct object)*, *infinitive—noun (object of preposition)*, *infinitive—noun (predicate noun)*, *infinitive—adjective*, and *infinitive—adverb*. The leader shuffles the cards and places them face down near the spinner.

How to play
1. Each player takes a turn spinning the spinner and moving the designated number of spaces, landing on a space with a verb or the word VERBAL. The player then picks a card from the deck and must write a sentence in which the verb is used as indicated on the card. For example, if a player lands on the space labeled with the verb *travel* and draws the card *gerund—subject*, he or she could write the sentence *Traveling is fun*.
2. The player reads the sentence aloud. If other players challenge it, the leader decides whether or not the verb is used correctly. A player who is wrong must move back 3 spaces.
3. Any player who lands on a VERBAL space gets another spin.
4. The first player to reach the finish line is the winner.

Variation
A simpler version of the game can be played by writing sentences in which the verb is used as a participle, gerund, or infinitive. Players can ignore such designations as *subject*, *direct object*, and *predicate noun*.

Verbal Race Track

Verbal Race Track

improve	draw	write	**VERBAL**	turn	excite	advertise
hear						help
VERBAL		surprise	fall	lead		encourage
laugh		pay		graze		practice
summarize		**VERBAL**		amaze		perform
disrupt		chill		**START**		travel
whisper		break				**VERBAL**
grow		return	run	suffer	sing	walk
FINISH LINE						

VERBAL cards

3	0
2	1
5	2
4	3

Dear Parent,

Your child is beginning a language and usage unit on clauses. In this unit of HOUGHTON MIFFLIN ENGLISH, your child will learn first to recognize and correctly punctuate different kinds of clauses and then to use the correct forms of relative pronouns. While practicing joining related ideas into sentences in a number of ways, your child will achieve variety and clarity in his or her writing.

You can help reinforce the skills your child is learning by doing the activity below or by making up a related one.

Family Activity

- The next time you are planning an outing with your child, ask him or her to suggest places to visit. Ask your child to use subordinate clauses in sentences that give reasons for visiting these places. (A subordinate clause has a subject and a predicate but does not express a complete thought: *because I like it.*) Your child may express sentences like these: **Since I need a new sweater,** *let's go shopping. I'd like to go to the art museum* **because there is an interesting exhibit there.**

If you have any questions on the skills or activities covered in this unit, please feel free to contact me.

Sincerely,

Unit 14 • Parent Letter

Estimado padre o madre,

Su hijo o hija comienza una unidad de gramática sobre las cláusulas. En esta unidad de HOUGHTON MIFFLIN ENGLISH, él o ella aprenderá a reconocer los diferentes tipos de cláusula y a usar en ellas la puntuación correcta y la forma correcta de los pronombres relativos. Al aprender cómo juntar ideas relacionadas en una sola oración de diferentes maneras, su hijo o hija logará escribir con variedad y claridad.

Usted puede reforzar las destrezas que aprende su hijo o hija, llevando a cabo la siguiente actividad o creando una relacionada a ésta.

Actividad para la familia

- La próxima vez que planifique salir de la casa con su hijo o hija, pídale que le sugiera algún lugar para visitar. Pídale que use cláusulas subordinadas en oraciones que ofrezcan razones para visitar estos lugares. (Una cláusula subordinada tiene un sujeto y un predicado, pero no expresa una idea completa: *Because I like it* —Porque me gusta.) Su hijo o hija podrá expresar oraciones como las siguientes: *Since I need a new sweater, let's go shopping.* (Como necesito un suéter nuevo, vamos de compras.) *I'd like to go to the art museum because there is an interesting exhibit there.* (Me gustaría ir al museo de artes porque hay una exhibición interesante ahí.)

Si usted tiene alguna pregunta sobre las destrezas o actividades que se presentan en esta unidad, por favor sienta la libertad de comunicarse conmigo.

Sinceramente,

Unit 14 • Parent Letter

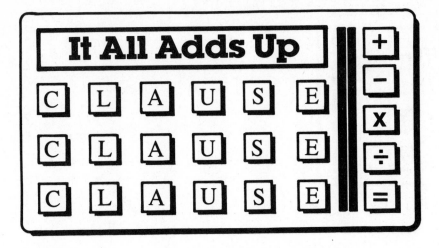

Objective
To add clauses to sentences

Players
2–6

You will need
Index cards; a scorecard (on the next page)

Before you play
Each player takes 2 or 3 cards and writes on each card the name of a subject, such as a nation, an historical figure, a performer, an artist, a planet, a tool, a machine, an animal, an event, an occupation, or a landmark. Shuffle all the cards, and place them face down in a pile. Also choose a scorekeeper who is also judge.

How to play
1. The first player draws a card and creates a sentence about the designated subject. For example, if the subject is Ernest Hemingway, the player might say, "Ernest Hemingway is a novelist."
2. The second player must add a clause to that sentence. For example, the player could say, "Ernest Hemingway is a novelist whom I greatly admire."
3. The third player must add another clause to the sentence, as in the following example: "Although some of his subjects are unfamiliar to me, Ernest Hemingway is a novelist whom I greatly admire."
4. Players take turns until someone is unable to add a clause or until all players have had 1 turn. The next player then draws another card from the deck, and the game continues.
5. If a player's clause is challenged, the scorekeeper decides if points will be awarded.

Scoring
A player earns 1 point for each clause added to the original sentence. If the player can identify the clause as a noun clause, an adjective clause, or an adverb clause, he or she earns an additional point. The player with the most points is the winner.

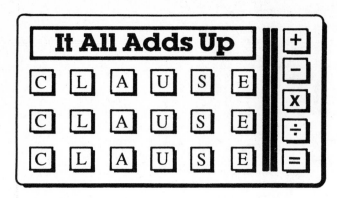

Scorecard

Player	1	2	3	4	5	6
Clause added						
Clause identified						
Points						
Clause added						
Clause identified						
Points						
Clause added						
Clause identified						
Points						
Clause added						
Clause identified						
Points						
Clause added						
Clause identified						
Points						
Total Points						